Enhancing Exercise Motivation

A Guide to Increasing
Fitness Center Member Retention

Dr. James J. Annesi

A FITNESS MANAGEMENT BOOK
Leisure Publications, Inc., Los Angeles, California
1996

ISBN: 0-9652432-0-6

Cartoons by Jim Whiting
Managing Editor: Ronale Tucker
Associate Editor: Christina Gandolfo
Editorial Assistant: H. Claire Jackson
Design, typography, graphics: Ed Pitts
Production Manager: Pamela S. Frankhauser

Published by:

FITNESS MANAGEMENT Magazine
an operating division of
Leisure Publications, Inc.

Corporate & Sales Offices
3923 West Sixth Street
Los Angeles, CA 90020
Telephone: 213 385-3926
Fax: 213 385-3920
Email: fitmgt@earthlink.net

Editorial & Permissions Offices
215 So. Highway 101, Suite 110
P.O. Box 1198
Solana Beach, CA 92075
Telephone: 619 481-4155
Fax: 619 481-4228
Email: fitmgt@cts.com

WorldWide Web site: http://www.fitnessworld.com

Printed in the United States of America

10   9   8   7   6   5   4   3   2   1

Contents

Preface

IT IS CLEAR THAT our present culture validates regular exercise. What was once viewed as a leisure pursuit has evolved into an essential element for total well-being. The media portrays exercise as providing health promotion, stress reduction, disease prevention and weight controlling properties. The surgeon general advocates that regular, vigorous activity be built into everyone's lifestyle. Why, then, have the exercise goals set by the government not nearly been met? Why do exercise dropout rates usually exceed 50 percent within six months of starting a program? What impact does this have on fitness facilities whose very existence depends upon getting, and keeping, members exercising?

In this book you will learn what factors have long-term influence on people's exercise habits. It is directed at fitness center administrators and professionals who can make a monumental difference in facilitating maintained exercise for their clients and, in turn, promote their own facility's success. The focus is on nurturing the exercise habit and increasing retention rates.

Carefully conducted research has produced a full-scale technology of exercise adherence methods and strategies. Within this book, you will see how the products of scientific inquiry can be taken out of the research world, put into practical form, and used by you, the practitioner. Until now, such techniques have been left largely in the storage vault of academia. This book will serve as your step-by-step guide for taking the relevant contributions from exercise psychology, behavioral psychology, performance enhancement and stress management, and putting them to work for your immediate benefit. Exercise is treated as a desirable behavior over which you, along with your clients, may gain control. Strategies such as relapse prevention, goal-setting, dissociation from discomfort and motivational assessment will become yours to enhance exercise persistence and raise retention rates. You and your staff are given the necessary tools to affect change in a systematic, flexible, dependable manner.

As you embark on the fascinating and worthwhile task of understanding exercise behavior, you will begin to see the logic behind exercise adherence and dropout. As you review experimental successes, you will see how carefully designed and administered techniques can reliably improve adherence. As you discover how the implementation of a step-by-step, psychologically-based retention program gives you control over what was previously considered uncontrollable (dropout), you will begin to see your professional role take on new dimensions. Drawing from the guidance that this book provides, I encourage you to perfect each step of your new retention program within your own center, with your own staff. Rapid and continued success will surely be shared by both you and your clients.

James J. Annesi

1

The problem of exercise dropout

ALL FITNESS CENTER OWNERS, administrators and directors are familiar with the problem of exercise dropout. Although our entire population is reminded almost every day of the great physical and psychological benefits of regular exercise, dropout from exercise programs remains high. In fact, retention rates have changed little through the years despite well-meaning, albeit nonscientific, efforts to change them. It can confidently be predicted that 50 percent of individuals entering a regular exercise program will not remain through six months (see Figure 1.1).

A Technology for exercise program adherence

As fitness center professionals, it is important to know that substantial advances are being made in countering exercise dropout. However, much of this evolving technology has been housed within the exclusive domain of research academics. While exercise psychology researchers debate the minutely-detailed nuances concerning their controlled experimental efforts, the real world of private and corporate fitness centers, YMCAs and other community programs go unaffected. Through a review of years of fitness industry conference offerings, only one or two presentations dealt with the transfer of research-based exercise adherence knowledge to those needing it — you, the fitness center professional. This is surprising given that dropout prevention, or retention, was cited as the industry's largest challenge (IRSA, 1993).

Fitness program administrators, being largely physiologically-trained professionals, have not consulted research publications in exercise psychology because the ideas are often difficult to adapt on a practical level. The goal of this book, therefore, is to translate the body of research surrounding retention into usable information for the practitioner.

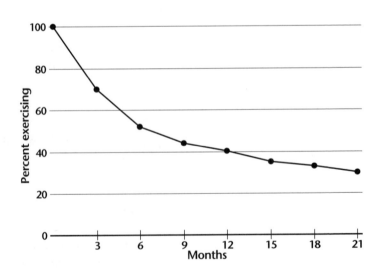

Figure 1.1. Expected dropout rate from an exercise program over time.

Preventing dropout: A systematic approach

Through this book, you will learn how to help clients maintain long-term exercise programs. Although individual motivations may vary for accomplishing this goal, you can be assured that your efforts are important. You will, in fact, be directly impacting the national wellness goals set forth in *Healthy People 2000* (U.S. Department of Health and Human Services, 1991), a national mandate that specifies exercise and wellness goals for the year 2000.

Through this book, you will systematically learn the nature of exercise behavior, its adoption and the nature of attrition. Understanding some of the theories of why individuals initially undertake exercise behaviors and subsequently drop them is key to developing a coherent system of action for reducing dropout. Also, you will be presented with important research findings that hold the key to developing an effective retention program. A major consideration in the presentation of these findings will be the ability to readily adapt them to your needs. In furthering the adaptation of exercise psychology research findings to your exercise facility, an actual protocol, or system, for your use will be outlined. This system has been field-tested under the name MAP (Member Adherence Program; Annesi, 1994), which has proven itself to be adaptable to various fitness center settings and effective in reducing dropout. As you will see, MAP's strength is in its ability to synthesize a substantial number of scientifically validated interventions, and present them in a package useful for administrators, trainers and other staff who are in direct contact with exercisers.

Research has shown that exercise adherence can be enhanced through psychological methods. In the following chapters, you will be given tools to accurately assess psychological make-ups and use specific methods to enhance and repair the ability to persist. You may be amazed at the technology available to enhance motivation, minimize exercise dis-

3

comfort and boredom, and move clients' new exercise experiences into beneficial habits.

Additionally, considerable time will be spent detailing how to implement the system to fit your own environment and conditions. Critical techniques, such as psychological assessment, goal setting, contracting and social support will be presented.

Learning from past shortcomings

To effectively undertake the challenge of helping clients adhere to exercise, it is important to review the fitness industry's past efforts. Since scientific research has not, until now, been used to direct large-scale retention efforts, intuition had to be used in lieu of formally tested knowledge. As you have probably guessed by now, it is my opinion that research-based knowledge is clearly preferred. However, both research and intuition can be useful. For example, fitness center supervisors have usually felt that a clean, pleasant atmosphere was useful in retaining their members. That certainly seems to be true. They have insisted that trainers and other staff be friendly. And while this seems logical, research has shown that only when trainers were rated as "poor," did it affect attendance (Andrews et al., 1981).

Trainers have often indicated that they can only help participants attain their goals if they come in with enough willingness (motivation) to "do it." This implies that many professionals view motivation, or the willingness to persist, to be an inherent, personal trait — something someone either has or does not have. Numerous studies have confirmed that when specific, psychological techniques are employed (this will be discussed later) and/or skills are learned, exercise adherence changes for the better. Whether "motivation" actually was changed is not really our concern; exercise behavior changed. You must be able to convince staff that their directed efforts will be useful.

In a similar light, some trainers claim the ability to predict a client's likeliness to drop out by the attitude he or she projects. Some have said that a "bad attitude" toward exercise will surely doom a client to early failure. Research shows us that attitude toward exercise is not an important indicator of dropout (Dishman & Gettman, 1980). Such individuals need to be fully attended to, as any other, by fitness professionals; not be given up as lost causes.

When a client starts a program, he/she is often "psyched" for action. Trainers often mistakenly take their cue from this enthusiasm and prescribe very challenging exercise routines. Unfortunately, a participant's initial euphoria usually does not last long. Soon the stress and discomfort of an over-aggressive program overwhelms the client. As a result, they drop out.

Most fitness centers offer group aerobics and swim programs, but few offer group classes or programs with cardiovascular equipment and/or resistance machines. Since adherence has been shown to increase when groups are present (Spink & Carron, 1994), and since social aspects are a significant reason

Initial euphoria usually does not last long.

people continue exercise (Wankel, 1985), retention opportunities were surely missed by not providing such programs. As many as 90 percent of exercisers prefer not to be alone while exercising (Heinzelmann & Bagley, 1970).

If research findings had been used in the past, we could assume that many procedures within fitness centers would be different. Since the industry has not evolved an effective norm (given present dropout rates), you will need to be open to change. A willingness to be open to new methods, adapted through systematic research efforts, will result in great dividends to both you and your clients. This book will provide such methods.

Understanding the process

I have attempted to review our goal of exercise adherence, which will lead to better client retention. I have, hopefully, whetted your appetite for a more scientific knowledge base regarding exercise adoption, attrition and dropout prevention. In criticizing some of the methods common to fitness center operations that were based on seemingly reasonable assumptions, I pointed out some common flaws that research results have enlightened us about. It is my hope that this book may motivate you to redirect much of your energies to a different way of looking at, and acting upon, member retention. This book proposes a strategy based upon scientific research findings from the disciplines of exercise and cognitive/behavioral psychology, and presents it in a user-friendly format to be adopted at your facility. We will cover theories of why people start an exercise program, and what it takes to keep them exercising. This is a fascinating area of research that should be understood by every fitness center professional. To understand dropout prevention, you must understand the psychological mechanisms at work, and how they differ between individuals. Chapter 2 will present major models of exercise behavior adoption so that a clear conceptual framework is present on which you may base your exercise adherence enhancement methods.

Chapter 3 will review exercise psychology research findings that will impact how you keep your clients exercising long-term. The majority of this critical information has, up to this point, been of concern only to academicians. Attrition reduction techniques are diverse in scope. Some serve to evaluate a client's likelihood of dropping out; some suggest specific goal-setting methods that enhance motivation and interest, while keeping discomfort to a minimum. Others describe proven methods, through painstaking experimental efforts, which increase a participant's perception of vitality, accomplishment and social support to reinforce continued exercise. Techniques that have been used, as well as the results drawn, have been impeccably documented. We, fortunately, can be confident of their real effects on exercise adherence. Chapter 3 serves to review these important research findings.

Chapter 4 presents a retention system for practical use, based on relevant research findings. You will be guided through the use of the MAP system for member retention. This system utilizes knowledge gained through scientific experimentation, and adapts that knowledge into a protocol to be used immediately in your retention efforts. Methods for assessing client motivational makeup, so that staff attention may be tailor-made, will also be presented. Adaptations will be made to experimental goal-setting strategies so that this important ingredient will be at work for you. The establishment of a manageable, but challenging exercise prescription will be outlined based upon your knowledge of each individual's psychological make-up and goals, as well as physiological characteristics.

You will learn how to implement feedback and tracking systems that reward client persistence. Methods for implementing the important aspects of social support, self-reinforcement and self-monitoring will be systematically added to your other retention tools. Since research has indicated that problems associated with exercise discomfort often cause dropout, you will employ techniques that have demonstrated success in this area. Your clients will possess the skills to relax and distance themselves from discomfort while exercising. They will learn to implement positive imagery, which links exercise with enjoyable feelings. The important work with relapse prevention, or preparing clients for "slips," is another example in which experimental successes will translate into your clients' enhanced maintenance of their exercise regimens.

Chapter 5 will give you the needed skills for putting in place your own state-of-the-art retention system. All the specifics needed for training staff, tracking members and adapting the program for special conditions and special populations will be considered. You will be aware of how the sequencing of methods affects client success, as well as how each individual's makeup requires adaptation for best results. You will be clear on how to employ the latest research in exercise adherence to your best benefit.

Chapter 6 concludes with a review of why people exercise and dropout, what research demonstrates to be effective methods for exercise adherence, and how to adapt and implement methods right for your situation.

Throughout the book you will note a series of key facts. These were designed to quickly consolidate important information. They will serve as useful cross-checks when you are involved in actually upgrading your retention program and serving to enhance your clients' quality of life through continued regular exercise.

KEY FACT

1

Exercise is a behavior. Like any other behavior, it can be analyzed and improved upon through methods sensitive to each individual's psychological makeup.

2

Determinants of exercise adoption, dropout and adherence

GIVEN THE KNOWLEDGE of how regular exercise enhances health and psychological well-being, it may seem strange that more people do not exercise regularly. Such knowledge regarding wellness may influence exercise behaviors somewhat, but many other factors are also at work. This chapter will explain some possible reasons why people begin to exercise, why some continue and why many drop out. The whos, wheres and whys surrounding exercise participation are not easy to answer. Psychologists hold vastly differing perspectives on the subject.

Within this book, exercise is treated as a behavior. We will ultimately be seeking to help alter behavior patterns of your clients by using strategies and methods proven to be beneficial. Generally, these methods will fit around theoretical models of exercise adoption and retention. As we review some of the most important models in widespread use in research today, you will begin to see the complexities of the exercise adherence problem unfold. You will notice how many factors you have to account for in the development of a retention system that works well.

As you read about the models, case examples will be added to enhance your understanding. You, no doubt, will think of your own examples of why one theory may be more relevant than others concerning certain types of clients. Try to pick out the salient features of each, as these are what your ultimate treatment design for the dropout problem will be based upon. Notice that some theorists look at exercise behavior as being controlled by education, while others see it as more influenced by social pressures. Some will propose that an individual's ability to plan and reason controls exercise behavior, while others view it as a cost-vs.-benefits problem.

Your review of these theories will allow you to understand and employ dropout prevention interventions with confidence, based on an increased understanding of the mechanisms that are controlling client actions.

Exercise adoption

To best understand exercise dropout, we will first review and simplify theories of exercise participation. As you learn what keeps people exercising, you will begin to perceive what mechanisms may fail, causing people to drop out. Your control over these failures can keep your clients exercising long-term. Review these models with this in mind.

THE EXERCISE BEHAVIOR MODEL

Noland and Feldman (1984) produced a comprehensive model regarding a person's likeliness to exercise. Four preconditions for readiness to exercise were included: a) a person's perceived control over the exercise setting, b) their attitude toward physical activity, c) their self-concept and d) the value placed on their health and physical fitness. These preconditions are influenced by "cues to action" such as advice from others to exercise, exposure to others exercising and education about exercise benefits. Barriers that may be present include lack of time, cost, and pain and discomfort caused by exercising. This model is a costs-vs.-benefits system. If conditions are correct, a person will exercise as long as the perceived benefits outweigh the costs.

Often, when people come to fitness centers, they already possess the necessary conditions to start exercising. Using the Exercise Behavior Model, your job is to enhance the preconditions and maximize benefits, while countering the barriers. We have all seen the individual who appears motivated by all the "right" reasons. Emily was 28 and sometimes felt "tired." She was concerned with her health. Through education, she was convinced that regular exercise would both ward off illness and improve her appearance. Her family and co-workers supported her decision to join a fitness facility and begin a regular exercise program. However, after several weeks, she began experiencing discomfort from the demanding exercise program she had undertaken. Although she still thought her family and friends supported the idea of her exercising, they were not complimenting her as much as in the beginning. She also perceived a loss of "free time" after work. After a brief illness and missing a week at the gym, she cancelled her membership.

In an analysis of the above scenario (based on the Exercise Behavior Model), we see that barriers overcame the perceived benefits of exercising. Since Emily did not have specific techniques at her disposal to counter the barriers while enhancing the perceived benefits, dropout happened soon after she started her program. In the design of the MAP program (to be presented in detail later), specific methods will be presented to you so that clients' perceived benefits are maximized, while barriers and discomforts are minimized. The Exercise Behavior Model highlights the need to be aware of situations affecting a person's perception of benefits-vs.-costs.

PSYCHOLOGICAL MODEL FOR PHYSICAL ACTIVITY PARTICIPATION

Sonstroem (1978) developed this model based on the relationship between physical activity and self-esteem. It assumes that involvement in exercise raises a person's physical self-estimation. This, in turn, leads to overall higher levels of self-esteem. Because people with high levels of self-esteem take pride in how they look, they continue to exercise. Additional exercise leads to even greater self-esteem and greater attraction to physical activity. Thus, an ongoing cycle is produced.

When people begin fitness programs, their progress is often slow. A sedentary, 53-year-old male starting exercise will usually see only gradual changes in his body if an appropriate exercise prescription is followed. Through application of the Psychological Model for Physical Activity Participation, your job is to emphasize the importance of small gains. When the client links exercise with its perceived effect, it will lead to an increase in self-esteem and an increased attraction to continued exercise.

In my own consulting work, I have seen many cases that have exemplified Sonstroem's model. Joe, age 32, for example, had never been especially athletic. After joining a private fitness center, however, he began using weight machines and noticing effects on his body that he very much liked. He became more and more attracted to exercise — both cardiovascular and resistance — and now works out almost every day. His body language is that of a confident, self-assured person, much different than when he began at the center. Given his continued interest in his new appearance, and the self-confidence it brings him, he will probably continue to exercise long-term.

THEORY OF REASONED ACTION

This theory suggests that people usually act reasonably and use information available to them. It also assumes that people consider in great depth the implications of their behaviors before undertaking them, thus developing "intentions" that are the basis of behaviors (Ajzen & Fishbein, 1980). The determinants of these intentions are a) the attitude toward the behavior; that the behavior leads to certain outcomes (good or bad), and b) subjective norms; individuals or groups thinking that the person should, or should not, undertake the behavior. Both the individual's own attitude and other's pressures on him/her develop the intention that influences the behavior being accomplished.

Translated into exercise terms, a person develops goals that may reasonably be expected to be achieved through exercise. Initial and continued involvement in exercise is also affected by the social support and validity that others important to the potential exerciser hold. The Theory of Reasoned Action, while seemingly abstract, applies well to your quest of maintaining involvement in exercise. It becomes your mission, as will be detailed later, to clarify a client's belief that exercise will accomplish sought-after goals. Also, while society generally supports exercise behavior, that alone is not enough (otherwise, everyone would be exercising regularly). You should provide the means to initiate and maintain social support.

A good example of an application of the Theory of Reasoned Action comes through Pat, a 62-year-old grandmother undertaking an exercise program at a YMCA. Although her physician advised a light, but regular program of cardiovascular exercise, none of her friends exercised. She felt isolated and uncomfortable on the exercise floor with mostly younger, more experienced exercisers present. Her attitude toward exercise was that of minimal importance. While she usually complied with her physician's instructions, she could see no critical importance associated with her exercising. She received

15

little outside support for her exercise behaviors. Her daughter warned her that she should "be careful." Her friends showed little interest, not wishing to get involved themselves. The facility provided little in the way of directly validating her efforts, or providing for like-aged groupings that could have provided support. Needless to say, Pat did not last long with her exercise program.

Ajzen (1985) extended the Theory of Reasoned Action by introducing the variable of control as a predictor of behavior. Control is influenced by the factors that may interfere with the intent to perform a behavior. It is easy to see how problems such as deficiencies in skills, knowledge, time allocation and a dependence on others can affect the accomplishment of regular exercise. This theory, named the Theory of Planned Behavior, sensitizes us to the need for helping clients maintain a sense of control in order to maximize their likeliness for success. Many of the skills needed to maximize control will be provided for and tracked through the MAP system. It should be your intent to empower clients to maintain control over their own exercise behaviors, while supplying methods that support that control.

She felt isolated and uncomfortable on the exercise floor with mostly younger, more experienced exercisers present.

THEORY OF INTERPERSONAL BEHAVIOR

In contrast to the Theory of Reasoned Action, the Theory of Interpersonal Behavior (Triandis, 1977) suggests that behaviors are not always the result of reasoned analysis and social pressures alone. The habit of performing a behavior is also important. Triandis, the theory's developer, proposed that the conditions encouraging or discouraging a behavior interact with both a person's intent to act, as well as the habit formed concerning the behavior (how many times the behavior has been undertaken). Some behaviors become automatic and will be performed with little need for decision-making.

A good example of the Theory of Interpersonal Behavior used for analysis is with the case of Tom, a 29-year-old single professional. Every Monday and Thursday, he completes work early, around 4 p.m., and goes directly to his fitness center. He meets with several close friends who also work out at the same facility by 5:00 p.m. Between 6:30 p.m. and 7 p.m. they go out for dinner. This routine has been in place for about two years. It would take an unusual event, such as Tom's occasional work travel, to interfere with his well-developed routine. Little conscious thought goes into enacting his exercise routine on Mondays and Thursdays.

The role of routine or habit is important when attempting to help clients maintain exercise behaviors. When you can help clients establish exercise as a natural course of a day, rather than a decision that must be weighed and balanced, you have provided a great service to them. Often, little more is needed than to examine which events will trigger exercise (as was Tom's early workday ending) and which events reinforce exercise (as was Tom's association with his friends). It is great when these conditions happen spontaneously, but as a fitness professional, you will often be needed to encourage habit formation through strategizing with clients. The Theory of Interpersonal Behavior is important because it reminds us that not only is reasoned intention important, but that habits formed

17

by repeated, acceptable routines are also useful. Remember that habit formation plays a large part in solving the exercise-retention puzzle.

SELF-EFFICACY THEORY

Bandura (1986) has presented a theory of behavior that centers around an individual's perception of his or her self-efficacy. Self-efficacy is defined as a person's judgment of his/her ability to devise and execute strategies of action required to attain designated types of performances. Self-efficacy is believed to affect both the start and maintenance of a behavior, and define which activities persons choose to undertake, as well as how much effort and how long they will persist, despite barriers and obstacles. Individuals tend to undertake activities if they feel the activities are within their capabilities. On the other hand, they avoid situations that they perceive they cannot handle.

Since self-efficacy seems useful for our purposes, we must understand what it is comprised of. Bandura (1977) hypothesized that self-efficacy is made up of four factors: performance accomplishments, vicarious experience, verbal persuasion and physiological states. How you can best provide for each factor for your clients will greatly influence their maintenance of exercise, according to self-efficacy theory.

Performance accomplishments

Performance accomplishments are thought to be especially important sources of efficacy. Success with exercise increases a client's sense of mastery. Validating clients' efforts, to the point of their perception of mastery, is a critical element for enhancing self-efficacy and providing for long-term continuation of exercise.

Vicarious experience

Vicarious experience involves judging the likelihood of

success through comparison of others' efforts. New exercisers should be introduced to other clients performing manageable activities, so that they may make a positive prediction of their own success. Be careful not to threaten clients by showing them individuals who are performing at a level that appears "impossible."

Verbal persuasion

Verbal persuasion appeals to the logic of an individual. If you can convince clients of the likeliness of successfully accomplishing regular exercise, their confidence will be raised, as will their expectations of success. Verbal persuasion is strengthened with the presentation of tangible strategies that further assure clients that success is likely.

Physiological states

This refers to the physical feelings of anxiety and tension associated with the fear of not being able to perform well. It is important that clients associate their exercise experience with a relaxed, rejuvenated state, rather than a tense, anxious one. As will be discussed later, you and your staff should have the ability to teach clients simple relaxation techniques. Their control over unpleasant physical states strengthens their sense of mastery over exercise.

Self-efficacy theory provides us a rich conceptual framework in which to work. It becomes the role of you, the practitioner, to help provide each individual with a perception of control and mastery over the exercise experience. The enhancement of the specific factors that lead to self-efficacy further specifies your role in maintaining exercise routines.

TRANSTHEORETICAL MODEL

This model has been tested largely with smoking and other addictive behaviors, but appears to be very useful for exercise, as well (Prochaska & Marcus, 1994). In fact, Project

PACE (Physician-based Assessment and Counseling for Exercise), a national, government-sponsored exercise promotion and prescription program, used the Transtheoretical Model for the development of its protocols. The model is a stage-of-behavior theory. It holds that individuals are at different stages of readiness for change, and suggests that interventions should be tailored to those specific stages. The stages are a) pre-contemplation, b) contemplation, c) preparation, d) action, e) maintenance and f) termination.

Precontemplators are people who do not see the benefits of exercise outweighing its barriers and risks. As an exercise facility professional, you will have little contact with these individuals as clients. Contemplators see the pros and cons of exercising about equal. Often these individuals will visit an exercise center, or obtain written information about it without joining. Preparation stage people generally perceive the benefits of exercise, but do not partake in it in a regular or systematic way. These individuals are often early dropouts from exercise facilities.

Action is the stage in which a positive change in exercise routine has recently occurred. This stage is also the most unstable. Large amounts of dropout occur here. Your lion's share of work in exercise adherence will be directed at clients in the action stage. The maintenance stage generally assumes that the exercise habit is in effect. The movement from action to maintenance becomes your major task where retention is concerned. The termination stage is when there is no temptation to not exercise regularly. Exercise becomes built into a person's lifestyle. Only a major barrier will prevent the routine from continuing indefinitely.

Although psychological tests have been used in research to ascertain which level an individual is in, your own viewing of their behaviors (attendance) is also a good indicator. One of the best elements the Transtheortical Model has to offer is suggestions for what type of intervention works best at which stage. For instance, pre-contemplators need to identify potential barriers to exercise and how to overcome them. Contemplators need to commit to a schedule of exercise. They need to have the potential benefits to themselves reinforced and be given large doses of social support. Action stage individuals respond best to varied and frequent sources of reinforcement for regular exercise. Also, training in relapse prevention, or preparing for the inevitable slips in their exercise programs, is suggested.

Examples of inappropriate use of the Transtheoretical Model's suggestions come to mind during some of my consulting with fitness centers. Joan, age 52, for example, was transferred from a physical rehabilitation program to a general fitness center through her physician's suggestion. She was given the OK to start exercising with no restrictions. Since she had not connected exercise benefits with herself, the pros and cons regarding exercising were about equally balanced. She clearly fell into the contemplation stage. Unfortunately, her exercise prescription was developed by an inexperienced trainer, and was based only on her physiological capabilities. The program was so involved, it became a burden to her. Quickly, the cons outweighed the pros regarding exercise. She lasted three sessions at the fitness center.

If Joan had been given attention sensitive to her stage of readiness, the story may have been different. According to Transtheoretical Model intervention studies, Joan should have been involved in developing her own exercise routine, based on what she saw as manageable. Additionally, if Joan had been introduced to other exercisers in the same stage and in her same age group, she may have received the social support and reinforcement necessary for a person in the contemplation stage to move forward.

Since most fitness professionals bring to their work an inherent love for physical activity, they find it hard to perceive why people have trouble maintaining regular exercise. These theoretical models present a framework for you and your staff to better understand the problem of adhering to exercise. You

21

KEY FACT

2

People choose to exercise, or not, based on:

a) the worth of exercise to them,

b) their perceived ability to perform exercise,

c) their self-concept and

d) their outside support for exercising. Additionally, their stage of readiness to exercise and the degree to which exercise is habit are also important factors.

can see that a balance between a potential exerciser's perception about the need to exercise, versus his or her barriers, plays a major role. Additionally, support systems are critical. In fact, psychosocial reasons were identified as the single largest reason for exercise dropout (Oldridge, 1979).

The above theories present global frameworks from which we can intelligently conceptualize exercise behavior. However, individual factors enter into the picture as we attempt to help each unique client maintain his or her exercise program. Next, we will look at research that can further add to our understanding of exercise adherence, on an individual level. It is through general frameworks as presented above, plus individual factors presented below, that helping strategies emerge and can be tested. As Chapter 3 presents techniques for adherence enhancement, you will understand how and why these techniques were derived, and how they will increase your effectiveness in countering dropout.

Individual factors affecting exercise adherence

Individual factors will add greatly to your understanding of the exercise adherence/retention problem. The upcoming review is limited to research that will support our ultimate goal — developing an efficient, effective program that you can use to help keep all of your clients exercising regularly.

DEMOGRAPHIC FACTORS

Simply put, age is not a factor in predicting a client's likeliness to drop out (Sallis et al., 1986). You should avoid biases in this regard. Additionally, gender is not an important factor in adhering to an exercise program (Sallis et al., 1986). Exercisers with blue-collar occupations are more likely to drop out than white-collar (Oldridge et al., 1983). Possibly, blue-collar clients will benefit most from your education efforts regarding the benefits of maintained exercise.

HEALTH FACTORS

A client's level of fitness at the beginning of an exercise program has little effect on adherence (Dishman & Gettman, 1980). Even more surprising is research indicating that persons who have been involved with an exercise program are more likely to drop out as they become more aerobically fit (Dishman, 1981). Most fitness professionals incorrectly assume that clients starting out "in shape" have a great advantage in maintaining their exercise programs over those in lesser condition. A similarly incorrect assumption is that those regularly exercising and making progress are more likely to remain exercising than others. Possibly, those who do not feel that they are unfit give themselves more freedom to drop out than others. Clearly, exercise adherence strategies are needed for clients in this category. Clients will be lost without correct, directed attention, even when things are apparently going well.

Obesity is linked with increased dropout (Dishman & Gettman, 1980). Exercisers in a greatly overweight condition have much discomfort exercising. It becomes difficult for them to overcome this burden long-term. Smokers are also much more likely to drop out than non-smokers (McCready & Long, 1985). It is important for you to provide means to help clients with obesity and smoking problems. Obesity and smoking's association with health risks and exercise dropout are clear.

PERCEPTUAL FACTORS

Both enjoyment (Oldridge & Spencer, 1985) and self-decision (Dishman & Gettman, 1980) are associated with increased adherence to an exercise program. People that have ample say in their activities tend to enjoy them more. We will be programming for these factors by allowing clients to set both their own goals and their preferred activities into their routines. Lack of time is probably the most reported reason for dropout (Riddle, 1980). Researchers, however, believe that this reason is usually based on the exercisers' rationalizations. Not "having enough time" provides an acceptable excuse that is hard to hold them accountable to.

EXERCISE INTENSITY FACTORS

Generally, the longer the duration of each exercise session, the higher the percentage of dropout (Andrew et al., 1981). Much of this is due to exercisers beginning programs at too ambitious an intensity level. This causes soreness, injury, and a dread of subsequent workouts. As mentioned earlier, your programming must account for clients' initial level of enthusiasm often being too high for their own good. You can counter this problem by designing programs that encourage a controlled progression of increasing difficulty, rather than yield to the clients' common wish of a "quick-fix" approach.

Generally, the longer the duration of each exercise session, the higher the percentage of dropout

The social aspects of your programming will affect adherence. While most new exercisers cite health and fitness gains as reasons for entering exercise programs, they usually cite social aspects as primary reasons for staying (Wankel, 1985). Social factors include the exercise monitoring staff. Andrew et al. (1981) determined that a lack of supervision while exercising leads to twice as much dropout when compared to well-supervised exercise programs. Although a top-notch staff does not in itself cause better adherence, perceptions of a poor staff can be a problem.

Most individuals prefer not to exercise alone (Heinzelmann & Bagley, 1970). When exercise groups are formed, small groups generally work best. However, large groups can also work well because of a client's ability to interact with many other exercisers (Remers et al., 1995). Exercise groups have not often been developed for fitness center floor activities. You will see how simple programming considerations regarding this will support a raise in retention rates.

Peers and family are other possible sources of social support for exercising. Family support, especially spouse support, is associated with higher adherence than with those individuals not receiving such support (Oldridge et al., 1983). You should have plans in place to invite husbands and wives to education sessions regarding the many benefits of exercise. Peers also have great possibilities for providing social support for exercising. If friends and/or co-workers can be brought into joint-exercise sessions, both will benefit. You know this, based upon social factors associated with exercise adherence, which were reviewed in the theoretical models.

PSYCHOLOGICAL FACTORS

It is no surprise that self-motivation level is the primary psychological factor of concern in retention. Self-motivation is defined as the general disposition to persevere, especially when outside forces are not there to help. Sensitivity to differing motivation levels will play a large part in personalizing work with clients. Since individuals low in self-motivation are more likely to drop out than highly self-motivated persons (Dishman & Ickes, 1981), your work is clear. You must facilitate both internal and external reinforcers (rewards) for low self-motivated clients. Internal reinforcers will come in the form of programming for a sense of accomplishment and self-worth for exercising. External reinforcers will come in the form of staff and group support. You will need to first ascertain clients' motivational levels (through accurate evaluation methods), then program for their success based largely on this information. We, as professionals, need to reject the often-held assumption that a low-motivated client is doomed to early dropout. While this type of individual is certainly "at risk," research-based interventions will give you the tools to help affect their success. This, after all, is our challenge.

Summary

This chapter's review of the theoretical models of exercise behavior, and findings related to the many factors that affect exercise adherence, have given you an understanding of people's adoption and maintenance of regular exercise. The models, which form basic hypotheses concerning exercise, are diverse in scope. The Exercise Behavior Model states that the accomplishment of regular exercise is based on an individual's costs-vs.-benefits analysis. The Psychological Model for Physical Activity Participation assumes that exercise increases self-esteem. As self-esteem increases, so does a concern for one's appearance. This leads to continued exercise. The Theory of Reasoned Action is based on the belief that both a person's expectations for success, emanating from exercise, and social support induce regular exercise. The Theory of Interpersonal

Behavior accounts for the formation of a habit. Conditions encouraging or discouraging exercise, a person's intent to exercise and habit (formed by past regular exercise) are central to this paradigm. Self-Efficacy Theory has successfully explained many behaviors in addition to exercise. Self-efficacy regarding exercise looks to an individual's judgment of his or her ability to accomplish exercise, given the barriers present that may produce difficulties. Finally, the Transtheoretical Model predicts a person's exercise habits by scrutinizing which stage of readiness he or she currently holds. Some evidence indicates that effective choice of a helping strategy (regarding starting and keeping with regular exercise) may be attained through knowledge of a client's stage of readiness.

Knowledge of the individual factors that affect exercise adherence is important as we prepare to implement a system for helping clients persist, based on their individual differences and needs. Important information regarding the impact of health, demographics, perception toward exercise, workout intensity, social support and motivation level on retention were reviewed in some detail. This information will be of great use to you. You now know of many variables that may control the adoption and maintenance of regular exercise. Although the models differ somewhat, all focus on individuals seeking to maximize their gains, while minimizing their discomforts. Your review of the personal factors affecting adherence extends this reality to an individual level. The development and implementation of the MAP system for retention consistently has sought to maximize client gains while minimizing their discomforts. You will soon see this unfold.

Next, you will review research projects that have implemented strategies to increase exercise adherence. You will see a fit, based on the theoretical models and factors affecting adherence just presented, for each of the strategies. Some will attempt to maximize a client's motivation. Some will focus on increasing social support. Other treatments will seek to counter the perceived negatives often associated with exercise, such as physical discomfort and slow physiological gains. Habit formation and affecting a sense of control will also be addressed.

It is from this problem-solution matching system that your member retention system will benefit. From the next chapter, you will develop an understanding of how the problems associated with adherence, when matched with scientifically-driven interventions, can be solved. You will begin to see how exercise psychology can provide answers to, as well as describe the problem of, exercise dropout.

KEY FACT

3

Many factors (health, demographic, perceptual, social, intensity) are associated with clients maintaining their exercise programs. Motivation level is a primary one. Exercise professionals can facilitate many positive changes regarding each factor.

3

Research applied to increasing exercise adherence

WE HAVE NOW COME to the point of reviewing specific strategies proven effective for countering exercise dropout. Many of these strategies have been "borrowed" from fields such as stress management, performance enhancement and behavioral psychology. All address major factors that enable exercise behavior to become an ongoing process for your clients. Since your concern is improving retention within your exercise setting, this review is limited to relevant research studies. For instance, while convenience of the exercise facility has proven to be an important factor in adherence to a program, it is of little use to you. There is no way, short of building additional facilities, to address this issue.

While one-on-one personal trainer sessions have proven successful by providing ongoing attention, support and continually revised exercise prescriptions, they are extremely time-intensive and costly, and therefore not appropriate to consider for large-scale retention improvements on an ongoing basis. As such, studies presented will concentrate on elements that you can effectively change and add. Chapter 4 will then build on this research to construct your own effective retention program. The MAP retention system, on which you will base your system, is derived from multiple research-based findings that have been adapted into an easily-used format.

As you become aware of the time-consuming work that exercise psychology researchers have undertaken, I hope you will be inspired to tap into this knowledge for both your and your clients' benefit. For convenience, I have categorized the research. The first category, *Assessment*, will describe successful attempts at evaluating individual motivational levels. Since persons low in motivation require more directed help to employ strategies for success, this is especially important work. Much of your ability to appropriately individualize helping strategies will come from this research that measures exercise motivation.

The second category is *Program Implementation*. Here you will review research on implementing balance sheets, goal setting, contracting to goals and psychological concerns relating to exercise prescription. *Performance Feedback*, the third category, is concerned with how feedback schemes, such as tracking and charting attendance, affect retention. The fourth category, *Support*, reviews strategies utilizing exercise groups and individual encouragement systems that have proven useful for increasing exerciser support, and countering dropout. Finally, *Coping With Exercise* studies are reviewed. This type of experimentation is concerned with teaching self-control skills, such as positive self-talk and "blocking" discomfort, to determine their effectiveness in countering exercise barriers and increasing exercise behavior's longevity.

Some studies have examined how different adherence strategies work in combination. These will also be briefly summarized. The MAP system borrows, similarly, from many effective treatments. A coherent grouping of varied strategies addresses multiple factors, each of concern to you in facilitating adherence.

While reading the various types of retention strategies, presented below, evaluate their individual appropriateness for your facility's situation. As you will soon see, most are easy to implement, and each has proven to be effective.

Assessment

At this stage of research, it is not possible to predict with complete accuracy who will drop out of an exercise program. Attempts at deriving this information have centered around various forms of psychological testing (often personality testing). Most studies have had only limited success in predicting retention. Because the trait of self-motivation — the general disposition to persist — seemed important to exercise adherence, considerable research has focused upon this factor for individual assessment. For your purposes, successfully categorizing clients, based on their likeliness to persist, can affect the amount and type of attention you give them.

Dr. Rod Dishman and his colleagues have spent considerable time researching the link between self-motivation and exercise adherence. They have made contributions, as well, in accurately measuring a person's self-motivation level.

A short paper and pencil test called the Self Motivation Inventory (SMI) (Dishman & Ickes, 1981) has proven successful in predicting likeliness to drop out. For instance, the SMI has predicted length of stay at aerobics classes (Thompson, Wyatt & Craighead, 1984), and athletic training sessions (Dishman & Gettman, 1980; Knapp et al., 1984). In fact, in the study last mentioned, the SMI correctly classified more than 80 percent of all exercisers when body fat percent (another dropout indicator) was also accounted for. Excessive body fat and weight seem to make exercising more difficult to undertake, even with considerable self-motivation present.

In the next chapter, you will see how the SMI is used to classify clients based on their individual self-motivation levels. Since most fitness centers must ration the amount of time staff can spend with any one individual, the SMI will provide important guidance concerning this. Also, since persons lower in self-motivation require special attention when prescribing exercise routines (so that their limited motivation is not overly challenged, resulting in dropout), the SMI will provide additional guidance for staff's support actions in this area.

Program implementation

BALANCE SHEET

Three experiments tested whether the use of a balance sheet (individual notations of both the pros and cons of adhering to a regular exercise program) would affect attendance (Hoyt & Janis, 1975; Wankel & Thompson, 1977;

Client is directed through the process of writing down perceived positive and negatives in regard to their exercise participation.

Wankel, Yardley & Graham, 1985). In all three, better retention resulted for the groups using balance sheets than those
not using them. Wankel and Thompson were also successful
in facilitating clients reentering exercise programs after being
inactive for at least one month.

In the balance sheet approach, usually initiated by a staff
member, a client is directed through the process of writing
down perceived positive and negatives in regard to their exercise participation. The use of balance sheets is very cost-effec-
tive. Possibly, balance sheets work because they bring to
clients' attention realities that they had yet to evaluate. As the
pros and cons of exercise are brought to light, motivation may
be increased for many.

GOAL SETTING

Goal setting has been used in many ways with successful
results, and it may be one of the strongest motivational tools
you will use in your retention system. Goal setting is usually
used by exercisers informally, so it has been difficult to assess
its actual impact. Some important studies have been completed, though, that evaluate its effectiveness when used in a
somewhat structured fashion.

Probably the most significant research to date concerning goal setting's effect on exercise adherence has been conducted by John Martin and his associates (1984). They found
that when clients set goals, exercise class attendance
improved. When flexible exercise goals were used, improvement was better than with fixed, rigid goals. They also found
that goals to be achieved in five weeks led to better retention
than goals to be achieved in one week. They interpreted these
findings to mean that additional time to meet short-term
goals creates less opportunity to experience failure, when compared to trying to meet weekly goals. Nelson (1978) demonstrated the effect of specific, challenging goals upon exercise
performance. It was shown that "do-your-best" goals did not

35

work nearly as well as when exercisers were committed to a tangible, measurable goal.

Locke and Latham (1985), two influential researchers in the area of goal setting, have made suggestions that are applicable to exercise adherence. They suggest that: a) goals should be broken down into short-term or intermediate goals to help attain ultimate goals, b) goals must be accepted by the client, c) challenging goals are better than easy ones, d) tracking progress is useful to remain committed to goals, and e) a plan of action facilitates goal attainment. They further identified steps to direct goal setting with your clients:

1) Make goals and subgoals measurable.
2) Determine how progress will be measured.
3) Specify time periods.
4) Rank goals by their importance to the client.

EXERCISE PRESCRIPTION

Exercise prescriptions must be based largely on established physical guidelines. Client physical well-being and injury prevention dictates this. However, psychological factors should also play a role. Studies have been published that evaluate psychological factors in exercise prescription relating to exercise program adherence.

Clients' perception of choice of activity is important for promoting continued exercise. Within a private fitness center setting, exercisers who believed that their programs were developed based on their own activity choices attended more classes than those given a standard program (Thompson & Wankel, 1980). The group perceiving choice also stated more intention to continue exercise than the non-choice group.

Training frequency, intensity and length were also examined for retention effect (Pollock et al., 1977). No significant differences emerged for clients exercising one, two, three, four or five days per week. Based on the previously cited research about the advisability of allowing for choice, adherence may benefit by allowing clients a say in determining their frequency of exercise. High-intensity interval training was compared with continuous jogging and a combination of the two. Continuous exercise was associated with better adherence. This mode of training was also preferred by 90 percent of participants. It was suggested that intensity should provide for a training effect, but not be so extreme as to pose a burden. Length of training also had an impact on exercise adherence. As the length of sessions increased, so did dropout. Researchers have suggested that exercise programs be designed to be no longer than 60 minutes, including warm-up and cool-down, to facilitate high rates of adherence (Pollock et al., 1984).

CONTRACTING

The notion of clients undertaking a formal agreement to uphold their established exercise routines has been well-examined by researchers. Oldridge and Jones (1983) demonstrated a substantial retention improvement when cardiac rehabilitation patients signed agreements to comply for six months with an exercise program, while recording their heart rate improvements. Epstein et al. (1980) found that contracts, which were rewarded by the refund of one dollar for each week successfully completed, improved attendance in the college students tested. Wysocki et al. (1979) also used a return strategy for clients successfully completing a contracted-to-volume of exercise. Clients were returned previously deposited personal items as they upheld their formalized commitments. Volume of exercise was significantly increased for those "contracting" longer than the experiment (10 weeks), as well as at a one-year follow-up point.

Researchers have cited various advantages of contracting such as: a) its clarity, b) its direct involvement with a client commitment, c) its being a public, rather than private, commitment and d) its ability to provide a basis for a client-based or institutionally-based reward system.

Performance feedback

PROGRESS INFORMATION

Clients commit considerable time and effort completing their exercise regimens. Information about how they are doing is an important motivational element. Martin et al. (1984) tested whether personal feedback or group feedback was better in terms of minimizing dropout in an adult running program. Instructors either praised the group as a whole at the end of class (group feedback) or ran with them and delivered information tailored to each individual (individual feedback). In the group feedback conditions, dropout averaged about 50 percent. In the personal feedback conditions, dropout averaged about 10 percent. Given the large dropout differential, it becomes clear that personalized feedback must be provided within your retention efforts. Feedback may be directed at clients' physiological improvements, goal attainments, effort outputs, etc.

ATTENDANCE TRACKING

Formal monitoring of attendance has been researched in two ways. Charting of attendance, done both privately and publicly, has been examined. Weber and Wertheim (1989) examined 55 women at a community fitness center. They were divided into three groups. One group was a self-monitoring group. One group was a self-monitoring plus special attention group. The last group had neither self-monitoring nor special attention. Self-monitoring groups were required to chart attendance on a graph, and return it to the researchers every two weeks, for three months. The attendance was similarly higher for both self-monitoring attendance groups, in relation to the control group. Most differences in attendance occurred in the first three weeks and were maintained in subsequent weeks. Research was further conducted to see if the extra staff attention, given a self-monitoring group, could have caused better attendance. Since there was no difference between any group on clients' appraisals of staff friendliness and helpfulness, the researchers were confident that the self-monitoring technique itself was a primary cause for increased retention.

Public recording of attendance was researched by McKenzie and Rushall (1974). These scientists found that posting of attendance for all to see reduced absenteeism, lateness and leaving early. Additionally, the swimmers tested completed more work when publicly tracked. Public recording of exercise information should only be conducted with clients who give their explicit permission, in respect for their personal confidentiality.

Support

Support of clients' exercise behaviors is a major factor in the maintenance of the necessary motivation to persist. Researchers have generally looked both inside and outside of the exercise domain, and at both individual and group means for support. It should be noted that research is developing that suggests males and females may benefit from different types of social support (e.g., Duncan, Duncan & McAuley, 1993). This information is only beginning to surface, however, and may benefit us in the future.

GROUP SUPPORT

People prefer to exercise in groups. Heinzelmann and Bagley (1970) found that almost 90 percent of exercisers preferred to work out with others rather than alone. Researchers have used the term "cohesion" to describe the critical element of camaraderie and sense of team that groups provide. Since many studies have linked high cohesion with increased levels of retention (e.g., Carron, Widmeyer & Brawley, 1988; Spink & Carron 1993, 1994), methods for establishing and heightening this sense of team unity has been the focus of much research. For example, King and Frederiksen (1984) formed groups based on their similarities in jogging times. Additionally, they completed some team-building exercises that stressed what they had in common (music, backgrounds, etc.). Jogging was twice as frequent in the groups with support as opposed to those running without any guidance on group formation or team-building. Massie and Shephard (1971) studied the effect of a YMCA group exercise program on dropout, in relation to an individual program based on the Cooper aerobic point system. Dropout for the individual system was 53 percent, and for the YMCA group 18 percent. Loneliness and boredom were commonly cited barriers in the individual program.

Carron and Spink (1993), key researchers in the field of group cohesion, have suggested various productive strategies to increase cohesion. They suggest for exercise groups to:

1) Create a distinct group environment. Develop a group name. Make up T-shirts and posters for group identity.

2) Develop group norms. Establish group goals. Promote a smart work ethic as a group characteristic.

3) Have group processes. Regulars should help new people. Develop a give-and-take program so all will benefit from exercise routines.

4) Establish communication, such as a rotation of partners to increase interaction. Work in groups of four or five, with each person taking a turn leading or setting a goal for the day.

The Group Environment Questionnaire (Carron & Spink, 1992) is a brief paper-and-pencil test that can accurately assess a client's level of cohesion at a given point. Most group/adherence research projects now use this test to evaluate strategy effectiveness for increasing camaraderie and reducing dropout.

As was noted earlier, this research review includes only strategies that can be used cost-effectively on a large scale. Therefore, research about personal trainers' effect on client retention is not presented. You should, however, realize that almost all of the interventions presented in this book can be easily adapted when, and if, large amounts of individual attention are possible.

Dr. Abby King and her associates (1988) used phone contacts at about two-week intervals to help clients adhere to their exercise programs. The phone contacts followed an initial 30-minute session that included instruction in self-directed behavioral strategies designed to develop control over individual exercise behaviors. The five-minute phone calls generally reinforced the use of these self-control strategies. This low-cost strategy proved effective. The study was especially strong because it tracked each of the 103 clients' results over 12 months.

Adapting to exercise

Many clients risk associating or "pairing" exercise with negative feelings. When this happens, they cannot effectively adapt, and soon drop out. While much of the previously presented research took a "proactive" approach in designing conditions to increase retention, strategies that provide for countering exercise problems and discomforts have also been prominent and successful. Therefore, each of the following treatment types tested sought to evaluate tools for countering exercise adherence barriers, either in preparation for or during their occurrence.

The term relapse prevention was originally used to describe the alleviation of individuals' "falling back" into behaviors thought to be undesirable for them (e.g., smoking, illicit drug use). Its meaning in exercise adherence is the prevention of falling back into non-activity, or into an earlier state of not exercising. Interventions focusing on relapse prevention generally focus on helping clients gain coping strategies that will reduce the chance of an initial lapse or stoppage, and equally important, prevent any lapse from becoming a complete withdrawal from exercise. Clients who perceive even slight disruptions in their exercise routines as total failure often drop out when such, sometimes unavoidable, circumstances occur. Relapse prevention attempts to alter this scenario.

Belisle and his associates (1987) studied 350 "beginner's level" exercise group participants over 10 weeks. Training sessions for the relapse prevention groups included themes centering around self-management, high-risk (for dropout)

Clients who perceive even slight disruptions in their exercise routines as total failure often drop out.

situations and management of temporary lapses in attendance. Attendance was moderately to greatly higher for the treatment groups in all of the classes tested (jogging, aerobics and pre-ski). Treatment groups also persisted better in the weeks tracked after completion of the 10-week program.

King and Frederiksen (1984) presented exercisers with written vignettes describing instances (e.g., exam week, vacation, illness) when missing exercise sessions would be likely. Individual coping strategies (countering negative thoughts, promptly rescheduling a missed exercise session) were subsequently practiced. When the relapse prevention treatment was presented alone, exercisers doubled their productivity, compared to individuals not trained.

Knapp (1988), after carefully reviewing the research concerning relapse prevention, suggested that clients be trained in the following skills:

1) Identify high-risk situations.

2) Improve ability to avoid and/or cope with such situations.

3) Emphasize the positives associated with completing an exercise session.

4) Plan for inevitable slips.

5) Set flexible exercise maintenance rules.

6) Choose enjoyable exercise activities.

DISSOCIATION

The strategy of dissociation refers to the intentional distraction from, or blocking of, physical sensations (often discomforts) during exercise. Martin and associates (1984), as part of a study that was reviewed earlier, found that an exercise group trained in dissociation techniques had much higher attendance rates when compared to a group paying attention to their bodies' physical sensations. At a three-month post-experiment follow- up, the attendance differences between groups were even more pronounced.

Pennebaker and Lightner (1980) conducted two experiments that supported the efficacy of dissociation when exercise persistence is the goal. In the first experiment, exercisers walked on a treadmill while either listening to their own breathing (an association technique) or to street sounds (a dissociation technique). The results showed that focusing attention away from the body was associated with less fatigue and discomfort. In the second experiment, running on a small track (200 meters) was compared to running on a cross-country course. Running on the cross-country course produced lower amounts of boredom and frustration than running on the small track. The researchers surmised that since the cross-country course allowed for increased external stimulation, dissociation from bodily processes naturally occurred. This occurrence was thought to be the basis of the lower amounts of boredom and frustration (clearly barriers to exercise adherence).

COGNITIVE RESTRUCTURING

This technique involves the individual's reinterpretation of negative self-talk. For example, a self-statement such as, "I'm so tired, why do I have to do this?" is changed to, "I know I'll feel great after I get going." Atkins and her associates (1984) used such a cognitive restructuring intervention, in combination with self-reward, for completing exercise sessions. Walking persistence for the elderly heart rehabilitation patients tested was increased, as were fitness levels. The improvements were maintained at the six-month follow-up.

Intervention packages

Some researchers have chosen to combine retention interventions to create a combination of treatments, or a "package." Studies incorporating such combinations are often treated as a single unit when evaluating their effectiveness. As you will see in the following chapter, the MAP system takes this approach. Until research catches up with practical need, and all of the many combinations of useful treatments are tested separately, the package approach proves to be a key method for increasing exercise persistence and reducing dropout.

In a very thorough investigation of three slightly over-weight men, Keefe and Blumenthal (1980) employed a combination of stimulus control, goal setting and self-reward. Stimulus control is a technique taught to clients that enables them to obtain "triggers" for exercise. In this experiment, individuals were taught to exercise at the same time and in a similar setting each day. Goal setting was based on a gradual increase (not more than 10 percent) of walking distance covered. Self-reward was based on successful completion of exercise goals. Objects that served as rewards were chosen from a list that each exerciser constructed himself.

Each individual maintained exercise over the full year of the study. Each gradually converted his walking program to a running program. At a two-year follow-up, jogging continued regularly for each individual. Each stated that he no longer relied on the self-reinforcement technique because he found exercise itself to be rewarding.

In testing the effect of an extensive exercise adherence package, Fitterling et al. (1988) utilized a combination of contracting, goal setting, stimulus control, phone prompts, feedback, support, dissociation and cognitive restructuring. Five adult females participated. Contracts outlined, specifically, what constituted adherence. Portions of a $100 deposit were returned periodically as parts of the contract were met. Goals were increased gradually as clients' tolerance for exercise increased. Stimulus control procedures included setting out exercise clothes the night prior to a workout.

Prompts, or "friendly reminders," were elicited from family members, and given by experimenters over the phone. Phone prompts were gradually reduced from once every one to two weeks to about once every four to six weeks at the end of the 12-week experiment. Personalized feedback and praise were given regularly to exercisers. Feedback included publicly displayed performance accomplishments. Support was additionally provided by those living with the individuals in the program. Experimenters periodically called these support-givers to ensure that they were giving regular encouragement to the exercisers.

The exercisers were also trained in the use of dissociation and cognitive restructuring strategies. They were asked to explain their strategies in use, and were praised for reports that they had used them.

All five women adhered very well to their three-times-per-week program. Intensity of effort increased gradually, but consistently. At the three-month follow-up, four women were still exercising regularly.

Summary

Although some exercise psychologists have questioned whether it was specifically intended, exercise adherence treatments address many of the critical issues inherent in the theoretical models presented earlier (Chapter 2). Since exercise is a behavior, proven strategies from other behavioral sciences have generally done well in contributing to the facilitation of individuals' exercise persistence. Chapter 4 will use many of the research-based strategies just reviewed in the presentation of the MAP member retention system. This system was developed out of what I consider to be the best, most practical exercise adherence enhancement methods available. This program will form a logical basis for development of your own system.

In summarizing our review of exercise psychology-based research successes, I believe it is possible to consolidate important inclusions for an effective retention program. These are:

• Client's motivational levels should be assessed to: a)

evaluate their risk for dropping out, and b) indicate the degree and type of help they may need to persist.

• Goal-setting strategies should be incorporated for all clients. Both long- and short-term goals should be set and reset frequently. Goals should be specific and contracted in writing.

• Exercise prescriptions should be moderate, especially with low motivated clients. Frequency of workouts should be manageable.

• Charts should be used to document attendance and frequency of workouts over time.

• Qualified and enthusiastic exercise leaders should be present. They should be willing and able to give individualized support.

• Groups should be available and encouraged for all exercise activities. Exercise leaders should encourage a group identity to increase feelings of belonging.

• Staff should make phone contacts and employ balance sheet approaches when evidence of waning motivation (reduced attendance) is present.

• Training in relapse prevention should be given to clients early in their programs to prevent small slips from turning into complete withdrawal.

• Exercise-caused discomforts should be managed by training in self-regulation techniques such as dissociation, cognitive restructuring and muscle relaxation.

KEY FACT

4

Research has demonstrated the effectiveness of *many* exercise-adherence strategies. Effectively drawing from these strategies is the key to the development of a successful retention program.

4

Developing a system for increasing retention

IN PREVIOUS CHAPTERS, we reviewed the problem of exercise dropout, looked at theories of exercise behavior adoption and maintenance, examined individual factors associated with ongoing exercise, and discussed developing interventions to promote retention that are based on scientific research. Now it's time to put your new knowledge to work. This chapter will show you how to effectively implement scientifically based methods into your own retention efforts.

You will be reviewing techniques incorporated in MAP (Member Adherence Program). This retention system, which utilizes assessment, intervention and follow-up, is based on much of the scientific research with which you are now familiar. It is my belief that "traditional" fitness center retention efforts have been flawed and, in most cases, have not effected substantial change. They have focused almost all of their attention on trying to keep members that have already successfully adapted to exercise. They continue to miss the main point necessary for high rates of retention, which is to reliably facilitate the adaptation process for each individual. While well-meaning, they have almost exclusively been based on intuition, rather than research-based findings. It is from a desire to correct this deficiency that the MAP system was created. As you will see, MAP incorporates research findings into a format that you, the exercise facility professional, can easily utilize with your staff to quickly and significantly improve retention.

In this chapter, the system is presented to you in a step-by-step format that incorporates most of the known successful exercise adherence interventions. Enough programming flexibility is provided so that all exercise facilities may benefit, regardless of size.

MAP's pilot experimentation was with a large (3,000-member) private fitness center. Retention was enhanced appreciably (see Figure 4.1). MAP has also been successfully used in smaller settings, and it has achieved success through personal training.

As you read each step of this system, you will note that considerable attention has been given to implementation.

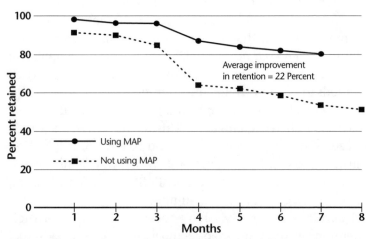

Figure 4.1. Retention results of MAP's (Member Adherence Program; Annesi, 1994) pilot project.

Methods will vary slightly based on your facility type. Chapter 5 will further clarify any implementation concerns you may have. Since each step can individually result in improvement, I have included a Key Fact after each to consolidate important information and serve as a cross-check when applying techniques.

Step 1: Assessing the member, anticipating needs, measuring motivation

Ascertaining clients' likelihood of dropping out is the starting point of the MAP system. The best predictor variable appears to be the personal trait of self-motivation. Enough experimental success (as was reviewed in Chapter 3) has been gained with the Self-Motivation Inventory (SMI; Dishman & Ickes, 1981; Dishman, Ickes & Morgan, 1980) for you to be confident in its use. The SMI will be used to provide a convertible score that will summarize each client's exercise motivation level. Clients with lower SMI scores will require much more care to enable success than those in the higher ranges.

A word of caution is needed before detailing the SMI's use and its implications for enhancing retention. Ethics in using exercise psychology inventories should be of highest concern. Clients should know what it is they are completing, and their privacy must remain protected. They are entitled to refuse to complete the questionnaire. They are also entitled to a summary of their results. Additionally, be aware that while the SMI is a useful tool, it cannot predict adherence and dropout with 100-percent accuracy. It should be used with common sense as a guide to how you may best serve your clients.

Specifically, the SMI is a 40-item questionnaire in which clients indicate how applicable certain characteristics are to themselves. Item scores are easily totalled, and a score from 40 to 200 is tallied. The test takes about five minutes to complete and about the same time for staff to score. When you obtain a

SMI score, you have useful information about how likely dropout is for any particular client.

Within the MAP system, clients scoring up to 110 are assigned a "1." Clients scoring from 111 to 130 are assigned a "2," from 131 to 150 a "3," from 151 to 170 a "4," and finally, 171 and over receives a score of "5." Clients scoring a 3 are about average in motivation. Individuals with a 1 or 2 are low-motivated; those with a 4 or 5 are highly motivated.

IMPLICATIONS OF SELF-MOTIVATION

As mentioned in Chapter 3, when SMI scores are combined with body fat and weight information, predicting likelihood of dropout is strengthened. Since your fitness center probably already attains weight/body fat data at intake, combining information will be easy and useful to you. For example, if a client falls into the "2" SMI range and has very high body fat, he/she is very much "at-risk" for early dropout. Special care needs to be given to this client to help with adherence to his/her exercise routine.

The SMI is usually given at intake when routine physiological assessments are made. Scoring is completed before the client's next visit with a trainer, so that appropriate provisions may be given in exercise prescription (a low SMI score would indicate a conservative exercise prescription is necessary), goal setting (lower SMI scores indicate setting more modest goals) and self-regulation (lower SMI scorers should be trained early in techniques such as relaxation and dissociation so that discomfort does not challenge their limited self-motivation). The SMI score has meaning for many aspects of your retention program. We will go into the implications of differing SMI scores as other parts of the MAP system are outlined. SMI score conversion should be noted on each client's exercise card. They are next to the space noted "I Code" in the sample (see Appendix A).

The Self-Motivation Inventory (SMI) is a copyrighted

KEY FACT

5

Assessing a client's motivational level is a key starting point for directing professional attention to individualized needs, as a means of maximizing retention.

test. The rights to obtain and reproduce the test are inexpensive, but must be obtained by writing to the address below:

Dr. Rod Dishman
Department of Exercise Science
University of Georgia
Athens, GA 30602

Step 2: Establishing client goals

According to numerous research findings, goal-setting may be one of your most powerful retention tools. The MAP goal-setting protocol includes research-based elements to ensure success by you, the practitioner.

THE GOAL-SETTING PROCESS

You should initiate your goal-setting process with clients at a second meeting, after physiological and motivational testing has been completed. The first part of the process is to have your client complete a Personal Goal Profile (PGP; Annesi, 1994). The PGP directions (Appendix B) ask the client to first note areas considered important (e.g., aerobic fitness, controlling body fat). A short list of common goal areas are provided, and the client is encouraged to fill in blank lines with areas of concern not on the list (see Appendix C).

Next, the client is asked to place a star next to the goal item(s) that are of special concern. Finally, a line is drawn from left to right, adjacent to each goal item chosen. Since "10" represents full goal attainment, a client's lines will correspond to lower numbers that represent his/her currently perceived status. For example, if "control overweight" is chosen as a goal item, is starred and given a line length corresponding with "2," it would be an area of great concern (and perceived need) for improvement. Subsequent goal-setting would reflect this. The advantage of the PGP is that exercise professionals are able to

obtain concise, accurate snapshots of clients' concerns and perceptions regarding their goals. It establishes a basis for formal
goal-setting, without being overly time-consuming.

The second part of the goal-setting process is reviewing
the PGP with the client. At this point, the exercise professional
clarifies the client's desires for health/fitness improvement.
Client and trainer should next formally agree upon long-term
goals in each area, and note them in a measurable manner.
For example, if "control overweight" is a concern, a long-term
reduction goal should be noted specifically and measurably
(e.g., 135 pounds). Document the long-term goal in the appropriate "Long-Term Goals" section of the exercise card
(Appendix A). For the previous example, "weight" would be
the correct category.

The final and possibly most important part of the goal-
setting protocol is to partialize long-term goals into lesser,
short-term goals. These goals should be set for two-to-three-
month periods. Professionals should negotiate goals that are
perceived as challenging, but are realistic. Clients with lower
SMI scores should be encouraged to keep short-term goals
manageable. Goals that require these clients to work too hard
risk pairing exercise with discomfort — a critical mistake not
often accounted for in the fitness center. Also, the inability to
attain a short-term goal that was set too high may lead the
client to associate the exercise experience with failure and,
again, overtax a low-motivated client's limits.

DOCUMENTING GOALS

Formalize the goal-setting process by documenting the
short-term goal and writing next to it a date for its attainment
(usually two to three months, at which time another meeting
will take place). This is placed in the appropriate box beside
"short-term goals." When this initial goal-setting process is
complete, each long-term goal will be documented with par-
tialized, short-term goals under them.

55

KEY FACT

6

Goal-setting is an essential part of your exercise adherence program. Clients should set challenging, specific long-term goals, and divide them into short-term goals. Short-term goals should be reasonably attainable.

It is important that clients: a) have a large say in setting goals, b) feel goals are challenging and worthwhile, c) appear willing to commit to their short-term attainment, and d) can see the link between attaining successive small goals and reaching their ultimate goal. The goal-setting process should be repeated every two to three months, especially for "at-risk," low-motivated clients. If goals are discovered to be too easy or too hard upon inspection of the exercise card, or through conversation with the client, they should be immediately reset to a more appropriate level. When you assure the client that exercise is a progressive, ongoing process, revising short-term goals is usually not associated with failure.

The exercise card is a central part of documenting and tracking goals. Headings for common goals and space left open for unique goals should be provided, as in the sample. Remember to allow clients the major say in setting their long-term goals, but exert enough influence to keep short-term goals appropriate for them. Be sure to document all goals in measurable terms (e.g., body fat, number of pounds), and be available to readjust them as needed.

Step 3: Developing and contracting to an exercise prescription

Many aspects of the exercise prescription are physiologically based. Your battery of physical tests at intake, along with guidelines presented by the American College of Sports Medicine (1986), allow you to work within the physical parameters that are best suited for each client. Within Step 3, we are concerned with the psychological aspects of the exercise prescription, or how the choice of activity and its physical intensity interact with clients' feelings of wellness, discomfort, overexertion, etc. By providing for these concerns, you may regulate the exercise prescription to allow for long-term maintenance of exercise programs. Since you are aware of the research findings concerning the relationship between exercise type/amount and exercise adherence, there is a firm basis upon which to proceed.

GENERAL ORIENTATION

The first part of the MAP exercise prescription is done at the same time as the goal-setting process (Step 2). When clients are either new to the fitness center environment and/or have low SMI scores, formal exercise prescriptions are not set immediately. Rather, the client is guided by the professional through the correct use of exercise equipment. General guidelines are given for amount of weights, repetitions, intensity settings, aerobic class types, etc. Although clients may often appear "ready" for an intensive prescription so that rapid progress may be made, setting a prescription too early is usually a disservice in the long run. As noted, clients often start their program with an initial euphoria that quickly fades. If the prescription is based on this heightened state, it will often be too much for the client when the initial enthusiasm wanes. Research has shown that when workouts are too intense, dropout is likely.

Additionally, exercise programs should be based on clients' likes and dislikes. Deferring the formal exercise prescription for several weeks to a month allows the client to "explore" the different areas of your facility and develop preferences. Also, the time commitment that he/she is able to realistically dedicate to exercise should be apparent by then. Set the formal exercise prescription appointment about one month after a client joins your facility. Set up the prescription appointment early, and follow it with a phone call about a week before. Assure the over-eager client that exercise is a process that you, together, are seeking to build into his/her lifestyle. This conservative approach will make goal attainment and long-term adherence to exercise more likely — a result you both want.

When the formal meeting time arrives, you will first review with the client their: a) exercise-type preferences, b) times they are available to exercise, and c) previously set goals. Add or revise goals as needed at this point. Next, you will begin developing their program. Use the information on the exercise card regarding goals and SMI level to guide you, along with the knowledge you have just gained about their time availabilities and exercise preferences. Together, establish a program that is sensitive to all these issues, as well as their baseline physiological measurements. Be especially concerned with short-term goal attainment, motivation level and variety when selecting activities. Remember that, while improving cardiovascular efficiency is a common goal for professionals to seek, programs should not be too taxing too early, or they will result in discomfort and dropout. Low-intensity levels, even those that do not rapidly improve a client's cardiovascular functioning, may lead to client success. Such a boost may initiate the exercise habit and continued, manageable intensity gains. Remember, research indicates that as exercise intensity increases, adherence decreases.

Document each facet of the exercise prescription on the client's exercise card. The sample card (Appendix A) provides spaces next to each element of the workout (e.g., weight, flexibility) in which both the prescription and each session's information may be recorded and dated. Additionally, include a short synopsis in the "Goal" section on the card that indicates which activity will contribute to which goal. For example, under the "Aerobic" goal section, inclusions such as "stationary bike 2x/wk" or "aerobics class 2x/wk" allow the client to connect their effort with a payoff. Document details of a weight-training program or stretching program, for instance, on other cards. As you can see, the exercise card is central for assessing, prescribing and monitoring clients. Clients should be encouraged to carry their card with them while exercising to enhance self-reinforcement, as well as give staff a better overview of progress.

Finally, how do you know the exercise prescription is a good one? The MAP system cross-checks the adequacy of the exercise prescription by using a brief (20-second) exercise psychology inventory. This inventory, called the Exercise-Induced Feeling Inventory (EFI; Gauvin & Rejeski, 1993), was designed to assess the feelings that go along with exercise. EFI researchers designed this easily scored and interpreted inventory to measure the feelings of positive engagement (feeling happy and/or enthusiastic), revitalization (feeling refreshed and/or revived), tranquility (feeling calm and/or peaceful) and physical exhaustion (feeling worn out and/or fatigued). By using the EFI when the prescription is initially tried, you can see how the client's important feelings are affected by the exercise session. While the typically used Borg Scale (Borg, 1985) may accurately measure perceived exertions, the EFI extends this into assessing how a client feels (positively or negatively) about the exertion.

The EFI is given just before and just after exercise. If there is a separate cardiovascular and resistance-training component of the prescription, questionnaire administrations should be done separately for each. Since research has indicated that exercisers' scores usually rise in positive engagement, revitalization and tranquility, and go down in physical exhaustion after exercise, you will be checking for this occurrence through your clients' EFI results (see Figure 4.2). A substantial deviation from the above pattern may indicate that your prescription aided in producing undesirable feelings in the client. If this occurs, you should confer with the client about his/her possible discomfort and/or consider modifying the prescription. Continual discomfort caused by a particular type or amount of exercise will inevitably cause dropout.

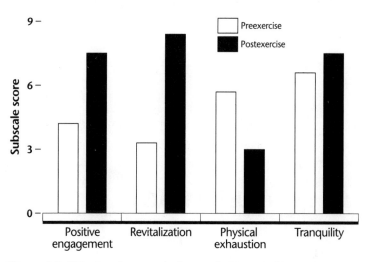

Figure 4.2. EFI subscale scores before and after exercise.

Source: Adapted from "The Exercise-Induced Feeling Inventory: Development and Initial Validation" by Lise Gauvin and W. Jack Rejeski, *Journal of Sport and Exercise Psychology* (Vol. 15, No. 4), p. 418. Copyright 1993 by Human Kinetics Publishers. Reprinted by permission.

The EFI, its instructions and scoring guide are given in Appendix D.

CONTRACTING

As noted in Chapter 3, formal contracting to exercise programs and goals has been associated with increased retention in research studies. To institute contracting with a client, first review the finalized versions of the goals and exercise prescription together. Make sure that they are adequately documented on the client's exercise card. Make any needed revisions. Next, agree with the client that a commitment is being made to adhere to the program. Be very specific as to what is expected. Finally, after all such issues are clear, you should each initial and date your agreement somewhere on the workout card (see "Contract" area in Appendix A).

If problems in intensity, frequency and/or activity type arise, simply recontract to the revision(s) and again date the

KEY FACT

7

After being given some time to develop exercise preferences, clients should be given formal exercise prescriptions that conform to their time, intensity, activity-type, physical and motivational needs. Formal contracting encourages a commitment to comply with the prescription and continually work toward goals.

signatures. Only the latest-dated contract will be in effect. Even if no problems surface, each scheduled revision of goals and exercise prescriptions (about every two or three months) should include the contracting process. A key to effective contracting is to make clients feel accountable for their performances, while also realizing that program revisions are encouraged as needed.

Step 4: Goal/progress monitoring

SELF-MONITORING

Research has demonstrated that when exercisers receive individualized feedback about their progress, adherence is increased. The MAP system provides client feedback on two levels. The first is through self-monitoring, again utilizing the personalized exercise cards. Notice on the sample card (Appendix A) that an area titled "date" is provided next to "activity." This area enables clients to track attendance. Since critical, early goals may be limited to simply attending a certain number of exercise sessions per week, this section allows for that documentation. When a goal attained is verified through such recording, it is reinforcing. Encouraging clients to continue using exercise cards cannot be overemphasized.

Another facet of self-monitoring is through tracking intensities. Increases in areas such as distance run or time on cardiovascular equipment are recorded under the date, next to the appropriate category (e.g., swimming, aerobics class) on the card. Detailed documentation for resistance training usually requires an additional page, and should be provided. Remember, every time a client records an activity on his/her exercise card, an accomplishment is acknowledged. It is essential that this type of reinforcer be provided. The connection between effort expended, daily accomplishment, short-term goal attainment and long-term goal attainment is consistently strengthened by facilitating and encouraging goal/progress monitoring.

STAFF MONITORING

Another way in which MAP provides personal client feedback is through a trainer. Since "reevaluation" meetings should take place every two to three months, personalized, professional feedback is continued. Increases in exercise rates/intensities should be commented on during this client/trainer session. Also, previous short-term goal attainment should be reviewed together. After the recent exercise history is evaluated, new short-term goals and exercise prescriptions should be set, as stated in previous sections. Each two-to-three-month reevaluation provides personalized feedback to the client from the professional. Feedback should be encouraging, but realistic, so that appropriate goals and exercise routines may be set for subsequent months.

Additional sources for client feedback can come from posters that describe optimal training rates (by age and heart beats/minute), normative charts for flexibility and body weight, and cardiovascular equipment that provides individual exercise session outcome. Clients are able to draw comparisons and gauge progress. Because research has shown the value of providing individualized feedback on progress, provide for and encourage this type of reinforcement. Always emphasize, though, that exercise is a progressive, lifelong endeavor, and *any* personal gain is worthwhile.

KEY FACT

8

Encourage exercise goal and progress monitoring by providing a means for clients to easily track their own accomplishments. Also, provide individualized progress feedback at regular intervals by exercise professionals.

Step 5: Enhancing motivation

The steps up to this point have assessed motivational levels, facilitated goal-setting, developed exercise prescriptions, contracted to them and provided means for feedback on progress. It has been encouraged that each client be treated as an individual because of his or her unique physiological and psychological makeup. Foremost, client motivation should be encouraged, while countering barriers. To complete your work in this area, methods to further enhance motivation are available. Throughout this chapter, each technique presented has its basis in documented research successes. Some of these techniques are delivered through your professional staff, and some through your exercise programming.

Staff-based methods

RELAPSE PREVENTION

Your clients have had to find time to fit exercise into their lives. Inevitably, circumstances arise in which changes in routine will not allow exercise to remain according to established patterns. Often, clients feel that when a "slip" occurs, all is lost. They often perceive their exercise routines to be an all-or-nothing experience. Preparing clients for slips in advance can enable them to incorporate absences without affecting their general persistence. Researchers have usually termed such helping methods "relapse prevention." As was discussed in Chapter 3, relapse prevention methods can be varied. Make certain each exercise leader incorporates a method with which he/she feels comfortable, especially with low-motivated clients. Relapse prevention interventions are best presented immediately after contracting has been completed. This way, clients will realize the balance between the commitment just made, and the flexibility they are entitled to when valid circumstances arise.

One successful relapse prevention technique includes presenting various hypothetical scenarios to clients (e.g., vacation, family illness) which will often interrupt an exercise program. After picturing these situations, successful recovery back into the exercise routine is then planned for and visualized. Other strategies have included encouraging flexible exercise maintenance rules from the start, and emphasizing the positives of completing an exercise session, rather than the negatives and/or guilt associated with an occasional miss. Although methods do not need to be rigid, you should incorporate relapse prevention into your system to prepare in advance for situations that require client absences.

EDUCATION

Exercise professionals typically are fully convinced of the validity of exercise. You should not assume that your clients are equally aware of the benefits of exercise. Staff should constantly use educational "tips" and facts to enhance clients' exercise experiences and give meaning to their efforts. Your most at-risk clients do not often feel an inherent joy in working out. To them, there are thousands of other activities they would prefer doing. By educating individuals about the benefits of correct exercise, you connect their effort with a payoff.

Research has shown that persons of lower educational levels are prone to higher dropout rates. If, through this fact, we deduce that less-educated individuals do not make a good connection between exercise and its benefits, our educational efforts are made even more worthwhile. Encourage staff to develop innovative methods in which education about exercise may be provided for your clients on an ongoing basis.

It is common for individuals to have trouble maintaining their original exercise prescription. Usually when this happens, clients will reduce the days per week they attend. Sometimes, though, the workout itself is more taxing than originally thought, and the client will begin to reduce intensity levels. Your exercise staff should monitor clients' exercise cards to check for missed days or other signs of inability to cope with the original exercise load.

Staff should feel free to make changes, as necessary, to accommodate for alterations in time availability, interests, etc. When such a change is made, and recontracted to, failure is averted. When the validity of building manageable amounts of exercise into the lifestyle is assured, clients will often continue feeling that a burden has been removed. Train staff to actively seek out and remedy signs of a less-than-ideal exercise prescription.

For most of us, it is a given that staff should be as encouraging as possible to clients. However, clients can sense when praise is given in a gratuitous fashion. For encouragement and praise to be of value and truly serve as a reinforcer to clients' exercise behaviors, it must be attached to what the individual perceives as something well done.

Staff should be trained, especially with low-motivated clients, to pick out the smallest improvement and compliment it. Rather than general statements such as, "You're doing great today," use directed phrases, such as, "Carole, it's excellent that you have been able to add another 10 minutes to your treadmill work in the last two sessions."

Research indicates that behavioral change occurs best when positive consequences (rewards) are paired with desirable behaviors (exercising regularly and improving). Since

KEY FACT

9

Clients' exercise motivation may be enhanced through well-directed staff and programming efforts. Providing for continued education, encouragement and exercise intensity checks are essential, as is preparing for the inevitable "slips" in attendance. Encouraging group support, variety, enjoyment and effort recognition are also key elements.

reinforcers like weight and inches lost come slowly, they are generally inefficient in convincing the low-motivated client to stick with the exercise habit. The exercise staff should, in a directed way, partially make up for this condition. Remember to make certain that a desirable behavior, however small, is isolated and verbally rewarded. Your directed encouragement is useful in enhancing persistence.

Programming-based methods

GROUP SUPPORT

It has been my experience that group support has been the least attended to and, possibly, most important aspect of retention. Research has shown that more than 90 percent of individuals prefer to exercise with others. Experiments on exercise group effects have consistently demonstrated much greater adherence than individuals exercising alone. With the exception of "classes" (e.g., aerobics, yoga), fitness centers have largely not addressed clients' group cohesion needs, especially in the highly-used cardiovascular and resistance machine areas of their facilities.

One primary MAP method used to incorporate a sense of group camaraderie on the exercise floor has proven successful. Clients were first asked if they would like some "extra help with a trainer" by registering for a small group "made up of people similar to themselves." This question was posed at the second meeting (after intake). Since this service was only offered to clients with an SMI (self-motivation) rating of 1, 2 or 3 (about the lowest 65 percent), this allowed sufficient time to obtain scores. Although all clients benefit from groupings, it was decided that to best utilize limited staff time, low-motivated clients would be focused upon first.

Groups were formed based on: a) time availability, b) age

and c) general exercise interests (e.g., jogging, circuit training, combination of cardiovascular exercise and weights). Groups ranged in size from seven to 12 people and met two times per week. During each hour-long session, the group's exercise leader (a member of the fitness center staff) first met with the group in a separate room. Introductions were made at the initial meeting and at any meeting that incorporated a new group member. The exercise leader began by leading the group in a short warm-up, including stretching. Clients were encouraged to relax and socialize during this time. Group members then headed to the exercise floor to pursue their workouts. Inevitably, group members tended to informally cluster together giving each other support, encouragement and generally interacting on a friendly basis.

Some sessions had special activities incorporated. For example, in one session, the group came together so that their exercise leader could explain a new piece of equipment and its correct use. Usually though, the staff member would circulate, monitor group members' exercise cards, offer encouragement and help as needed. At the end of the hour, the group was again brought together for cool-down activities. Usually,

The fitness center floor is often an area where a low-motivated client gets "lost."

socializing continued well after sessions completed.

This method served to provide group support in an efficient manner. Essential social elements were combined with clients' exercise experiences through their own mutual connection with one another. While groups such as aerobics classes and racquet sport leagues tend to develop support systems of their own, the fitness center floor is often an area where a low-motivated client gets "lost." An exerciser often feels isolated and uncomfortable in strange surroundings when, seemingly, everyone else knows what they are doing. Creating exercise groups based on clients' individual needs and similarities sets them up for success. Since you are now aware of the impact social support has on retention, provide for it through your programming on an ongoing basis. Once your clients form their own exercise-based networks, much dropout will be averted.

RECOGNITION

Clients often perceive great rewards when their accomplishments are presented for all to see. You have already reviewed several experiments that have demonstrated the positive effect of public posting of physical performances. The MAP system provides for voluntary participation in such public recognition programs. You, too, should consider developing exercise "contests" that will appeal to a large range of clientele.

Only your imagination limits the number and types of client competitions available for you to use. However, it is extremely important that individual differences be accounted for. For instance, a contest that simply rewards amount of miles logged on a treadmill, or distance rowed on a machine, puts the older and less fit at a disadvantage. If incentives are given for percent improvement at set activities, differences in age, sex and condition can be effectively controlled for.

MAP has utilized graphing techniques, based on percent improvements, as the basis of competitions (see Figure 4.3). In this manner, all participants are visually rewarded by their gains, whether or not they actually completed more work than their fellow exercisers.

Recognition can be acknowledged on a billboard or in a newsletter. By using an adjustment scheme, as just described, and recognizing personal improvement as the basis of success, even those clients in the lower exercise intensity ranges will have great chances for receiving both internal (within themselves) and external (from others) reinforcement.

ENCOURAGE VARIETY AND ENJOYMENT

Research has provided us with a clear link between enjoyment and exercise adherence. Many times enjoyment comes in the form of variety. Since one of the barriers to con-

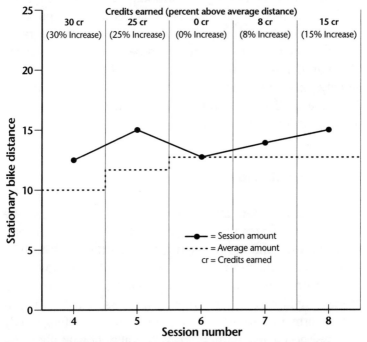

Figure 4.3. Tracking system enabling clients to earn "credits" for exercise completed above their own average amount.

tinued exercise is boredom, this is logical. Promotions and/or seminars that expose clients to new activities (e.g., racquet sports, swimming, yoga classes), without forcing them to make substantial time commitments, can prove useful. Including information about various activities, within newsletters and flyers also demonstrates a new activity in a non-threatening manner.

Try to provide means in which clients may observe different activities in action so that they can visualize themselves participating. Through this method, they can mentally "try out" many activities without initially committing to any of them.

Remember that variety can reduce boredom for the client; however, their sense of freedom of choice (of activities) is primary. Make certain that you expose clients to all that your facility offers. Provide the flexibility for them to mix and match activities within their personalized exercise prescriptions. Do not, however, insist that all clients try every activity possible. Encourage exercisers to "probe" to see what is interesting and enjoyable to them on an individual basis. Provide equally for clients who have found their "comfort zone" in familiar activities, and those in which variety will build enjoyment and a long-term commitment to exercise.

Step 6: Repairing motivation

Exercise leaders and trainers should not perform the functions of an exercise psychologist. However, they can provide a service, and aid in retention, when they seek to help clients combat their exercise discomforts in directed ways.

Efforts should be made to provide clients with techniques that block or reinterpret negatives associated with exercise performances to prevent dropout. Step 6, therefore, briefly outlines specific techniques, experimentally shown to be effective, that provide means for repairing waning motivation.

Altering the negative ways in which individuals may respond to exercise is done by training them in basic, comfort-inducing, cognitive-behavioral techniques. For ethical reasons, the techniques explained involve no direct counseling, and are generally acceptable and pleasing to most people. They call for minimal training for staff and, again, do not attempt to turn them into "psychologists." Exercise professionals should always explain to a client exactly how they propose to help them, as well as gain permission before using any of the valuable repair techniques suggested below.

DISSOCIATION

Enabling exercisers to distance their thoughts from the sensations caused by physical effort can be helpful. Experiments testing dissociation's effect on exercise persistence have concentrated on clients manipulating their focus away from the body during exertion. Also, scenarios in which there was increased stimuli surrounding the exerciser supposedly detracted from the inward sensations of discomfort.

You should encourage clients who appear uncomfortable while exercising to utilize dissociation. Simple provisions for dissociation include the use of a personal stereo headset, watching television or reading a magazine while exercising. Cardiovascular machines are increasingly providing screens in which exercisers' attention may be focused. Additional techniques include talking to a friend (possibly exercising nearby), varying activities so that the surroundings seem novel, and providing easy access to interesting reading.

IMAGERY

The cognitive technique of imagery is used, as dissociation, to purposefully direct attentional focus. However, it is accomplished completely within one's mind. Your staff should be able to give some useful guidance for facilitating imagery such as in: a) visualizing a pleasurable scene, b) reaching a goal or c) picturing an emerging, well-formed, healthy body. Also, in creating the image in the mind's eye, clients should be guided in: a) detailing the image as fully as possible, b) picturing the image from within one's self and c) developing an ability to manipulate an image as desired.

Helping clients to develop imagery skills gives them the tools to place themselves into a challenging sports task, or surrounded by cool tropical breezes, all within their imagination. Imagery has the potential to transcend the limits of what an at-risk client perceives as an unpleasant setting and task. You should possess the tools to suggest and facilitate the use of imagery for clients appearing overly tested by the exercise process.

RELAXATION

MAP has successfully used a modified version of progressive muscle relaxation (Suinn, 1980) to help facilitate pleasant sensations while exercising. Sometimes, when clients come to your facility after a stressful day or are tense while performing unfamiliar activities, they require directed help in relaxation. Remember, you are always aiming for clients to associate exercise with comfort and pleasant feelings.

When clients appear to be giving off bodily signals of excess tension, suggest that they try some simple techniques that will allow them to "relax and enjoy" their workout. Following are some steps that will help you to help your clients:

1) Ask the client to practice tensing and relaxing some of the major muscle groups of his/her body. Be sure to include common tension sites such as the back of the neck and forehead.

2) After this is practiced for a while (possibly for several days), ask the client to just relax or "turn off" tension, without first tensing.

3) Next, encourage the client to scan for tension-filled

areas, and turn off tension in those spots.

4) Finally, suggest that the above step be used while exercising.

Within a few sessions, most clients will feel that they have obtained a better awareness of, and control over, their physical anxiety symptoms. Muscle relaxation training can be facilitated within exercise group meetings or when staff circulates on the exercise floor. Relaxation training becomes another of your important techniques that serve to counter a potentially devastating discomfort for an at-risk client.

POSITIVE SELF-TALK

Often when conversing with clients, you may observe pessimistic patterns of interpreting the exercise experience. Clients' continued negative appraisals of their workout activities can be troublesome when long-term adherence is the goal. Staff should be equipped with the skills to enable clients to reinterpret their negative self-talk — replacing it with more positive self-statements.

When spotting a client prone to negative self-talk, suggest various examples of corrective reinterpretation. Advocate for the validity of such a technique to "convince themselves" of the many positives attached to continued exercise. A statement of dread (e.g., "I'm not looking forward to working out today") can be turned into a statement of opportunity (e.g., "I know how important exercising is to me — it's one of the best things I do for myself"). Self-talk expressing fatigue (e.g., "I'm so tired today — I'm not sure I can put in the effort") can be reinterpreted into a self-statement of rejuvenation (e.g., "Once I get started exercising, I always feel so much more energetic").

A technique called "thought-stopping" is also an aid in facilitating reinterpretation and positive self-talk. Tell a client to yell "stop" to themselves after observing any negative self-talk. The word stop then becomes their "trigger" to productively reinterpret the previous self-statement.

SELF-REINFORCEMENT

Often clients benefit when tangible objects, rather that simple thoughts, are used to reward the effort associated with an exercise session. Research has demonstrated that expensive and/or elaborate items need not be used, only objects/activities that provide a perceived reward for good work.

Your staff should train clients in methods of self-reinforcement when motivation levels are low, and/or effort appears to be waning. Certainly, your own creativity is useful in devising rewards that may be paired with exercise session completion. In the development of MAP, we have successfully used the following tangible self-reinforcements: a) allowing time for and taking a relaxing whirlpool directly following exercise, b) dinner out after a week of keeping with the exercise prescription, and c) a special item of clothing, for instance, after a short-term goal has been achieved.

Clients have the ability to look past the often taxing workout effort when a meaningful reward is to follow. In some cases, writing self-reinforcement arrangements into the individualized contracts has proven productive. Convince clients that it is desirable to reward themselves after considerable effort has been expended on exercise.

REFERRALS

Sometimes clients have needs that exercise alone cannot meet. It is important that you provide referral sources that can supplement exercise's impact on client wellness. Extremely at-risk clients may require the help of other specialized professionals to maintain the necessary motivation to keep them exercising long-term.

Properly credentialed diet/nutritional counseling professionals may be necessary for clients needing or wanting weight loss. Psychotherapists are often advisable when clients appear to have extremely negative body images, or seem to

KEY FACT

10

Exercisers at risk for dropout benefit from specific methods that combat their perceived discomforts. Selectively provide basic training in techniques such as dissociation, imagery, relaxation, positive self-talk and/or self-reinforcement in order to repair waning client motivation.

have a phobic response toward exercising in public. Physicians should be referred to when clients' physical limitations make an appropriate exercise prescription troublesome. Behavioral psychologists are often needed when smoking cessation is desired, and sometimes to supplement the impact exercise has on a client who requires directed stress management. Personal training should be available for clients requiring constant motivational supplements in order to maintain their exercise persistence.

Summary

This chapter presented major elements of the MAP (Member Adherence Program) system for fitness center member retention. MAP was built upon research findings that substantiated each aspect of the system. Major areas, termed "Steps," including: a) client motivational assessment, b) goal-setting, c) exercise prescription development, d) contracting, e) progress monitoring, f) enhancing motivation techniques and g) repairing motivation techniques, were incorporated into a usable treatment package so that experimental successes could benefit client retention in facilities such as your own. You, the fitness center professional, now have information on how to apply proven interventions, as well as when (and with whom) applications are most appropriate. MAP testing has proven it to be a system whose elements you may utilize with confidence through your present staff.

Step 1 is concerned with the assessment of motivational levels in the individual client. The SMI (Self-Motivation Index) is a vehicle by which client self-motivation can be effectively measured. Gradations were developed, based on clients' inventory responses, so that motivational level can be referred to when carrying out other MAP elements. Directives for making individual adjustments, when helping clients adhere to their programs, were discussed based on the implications of the possible client self-motivation levels.

Step 2 outlines the MAP goal-setting process. The PGP (Personal Goal Profile) is an efficient tool to: a) uncover client goals, b) prioritize those goals and c) discern how close clients perceive they are to reaching their goals. Directions for negotiating and establishing long-term and appropriate short-term goals with the client were discussed. Finally, the documentation and follow-up goal-setting processes were outlined.

Developing and contracting to an exercise routine are covered in Step 3. Directions were given to ensure that the exercise prescription attends to clients' psychological, as well as physiological, requirements. The EFI (Exercise-Induced Feeling Inventory) was described as a quick and effective test for assessing the feelings that a client associates with the exercise load prescribed. The EFI was suggested as a cross-check for prescription adequacy. Step 3 also includes directions for the use of contracting. Formalizing a client's commitment to an agreed-upon schedule of attendance and activity has proven valuable for increasing retention.

Step 4 provides methods in which goal and progress monitoring will enhance adherence. You and your staff were given the tools to set up progress feedback schemes that set clients up for perceptions of success and ongoing worth, associated with the effort put into exercising. Systems for client self-monitoring, as well as staff feedback, were outlined.

Enhancing motivation was the focus of Step 5. Staff- and programming-based methods, proven through research to increase motivation and retention, were reviewed and presented in an immediately usable form for the exercise professional. Staff-based methods included: a) relapse prevention — a technique to prepare clients for occasional "slips" in their attendance, b) education — to keep clients aware of the validity of exercise, c) exercise prescription modification — changing an overly taxing or time-consuming routine, and d) encouragement — effectively reinforcing clients, based on the effort and accomplishment that they have demonstrated.

81

Programming-based methods included: a) group support — developing supportive friendship networks within your fitness center, b) recognition — methods to reward clients based on their abilities, and c) providing for variety and enjoyment — introducing varied forms of exercise to keep interest and pleasure alive.

Step 6 outlines various methods which repair waning motivation. Since dropout is often caused by the discomfort associated with exercise, you were provided methods which can, in a directed manner, counter these discomforts. The techniques that were outlined for helping clients included: a) dissociation — training clients in skills that distance uncomfortable bodily sensations from their exercise experiences, b) imagery — guiding clients in the skills of visualizing a pleasurable scene, reaching a goal, or being a participant in a sport competition while exercising, c) relaxation — providing specific techniques that isolate and alleviate muscular tension, d) positive self-talk — training clients to reinterpret negative self-statements into positive ones, and (e) self-reinforcement — suggesting to clients methods that provide rewards to themselves for small, exercise-related accomplishments. Also, Step 6 gave suggestions for the inclusion of referrals for clients with specialized needs.

Next, Chapter 5 will take you further into the coordination and implementation of your comprehensive member retention program. Since you now are aware of many of the experimentally-verified methods within the MAP system, full and effective implementation becomes your next vital focus.

5

Implementing your retention system

IMPLEMENTATION OF YOUR exercise psychology-based retention system is not difficult, but some organization is necessary for methods to be carried out in an effective and consistent manner. While Chapter 4 outlined major elements of the MAP system, some aspects necessary for its successful application require further clarification. This is not surprising given the newness of this systematic approach. This chapter will clarify and resolve implementation concerns. When you have completed this section, you will understand successful exercise adherence interventions and their research bases, and be confident in instituting MAP Steps into your facility.

Differing roles

Although the types of staff may differ among fitness centers, most facilities employ exercise professionals, department

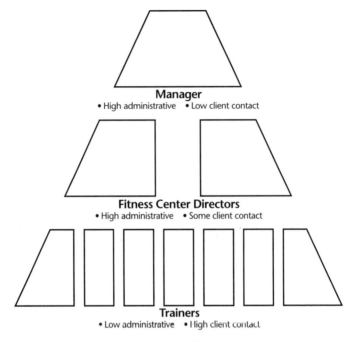

Figure 5.1. The relationship of the different fitness center roles.

heads and managers. Each plays an important, but different, role in applying the MAP approach to member retention. This relationship can be demonstrated in terms of hierarchy and responsibility (see Figure 5.1). Exercise professionals maintain the most "hands on" contact with clients, while managers develop policy, broadly oversee application and evaluate program effectiveness. Department heads are usually a "go-between," between establishing methods and assuring that they are effectively applied.

MANAGER

The manager, facility owner or administrator's primary role in implementing an innovative retention system is in: a) developing a consensus with department directors for what will be included within staff training, b) establishing times and policy for training session attendance, c) hiring consultants (e.g., an exercise psychologist) and d) evaluating the effectiveness of the program and making changes as needed. Managers should attend at least some of the staff training sessions to lend support "from the top." Encouragement from these individuals, known primarily for their administrative roles, can enhance the staff's sense of importance for undertaking their new and improved responsibilities.

An administrator's concern should be addressed to the effect a new program will have on staff performance, client service and retention. A wise administrator realizes that considerable planning and coordination are necessary for research successes to evolve into "real world" results. He/she should be willing to put in this worthwhile coordination time and become involved firsthand. A perception of serving both the clients' *and* facility's interest simultaneously should be maintained.

DEPARTMENT HEAD

The fitness center department head or director plays a critical role in implementing an enhanced retention system. Responsibilities include: a) coordinating with the manager and developing the content of staff training sessions, b) insuring that theoretical knowledge gets turned into practical, usable methodology within training, c) facilitating the application of new methods through demonstration and staff guidance, and d) evaluating staff members' success in applying the new exercise psychology-based system with clients.

Effective directors know each part of the system and why it is used. They teach by demonstration and are willing to present feedback to staff in an encouraging manner. The department head should set the tone for client service and an effective work ethic. Their single-mindedness toward the worth of long-term exercise and facilitating client success should be unwavering. They should require that all staff behaviors reflect similar concerns.

The exercise professional, leader or trainer is the primary facilitator of the MAP Steps. His/her role in implementing the system is to: a) learn each element of the system and, at least broadly, its research basis, b) know how to effectively utilize the MAP elements with clients, c) know how to adapt interventions to individual needs, and d) be willing to actively seek out "at-risk" clients and apply appropriate techniques.

The exercise professional should respect the worth of each client to improve him/herself through exercise. While usually being trained in physiological (rather than psychological) methods, an effective exercise professional realizes that *no* improvement is possible after dropout. Therefore, the validity of applying psychologically based methods, proven effective for improving client retention, should be apparent. Exercise professionals should perceive that a *major* portion of their job is to enhance client motivation through utilizing their newly developed skills.

Establishing a time frame

The order in which the MAP Steps are implemented with clients is significant. Since assessing client motivation is a basis for further Steps, it begins first. Goal-setting is next, followed by the exercise prescription process, which is affected by both client goals and motivational level. After these elements are in place, an effective feedback system that gives clients reinforcing information about their progress is put into effect. Steps 5 and 6 — enhancing and repairing motivation treatments, respectively — are implemented with clients during trainers' on-floor circulation time and during individual follow-up appointments.

Throughout the previous chapter, guidance was given regarding how and when to apply MAP Steps. This section will, therefore, serve as a review to: a) clarify the time frame for each element's application, and b) give you a perspective on the continuity of the system as clients' long-term exercise behaviors are maintained. You should notice how methods, designed to effectively initiate clients into exercising, move toward psychologically reinforcing and enhancing those behaviors. Finally, techniques are implemented that greatly increase each client's likeliness to "lock" exercise into a strong and worthwhile habit. Figure 5.2 will serve as your graphic timeline as you review when to implement the various elements of the MAP system.

The initial staff/client interaction is referred to as "intake" in Chapter 4. At that time, a trainer evaluates a client's baseline physiological measurements (e.g., blood pressure, flexibility) and history of disease and/or injury. The client is also provided with general information about the fitness center and its services. At the initial meeting, the client completes the SMI (Self-Motivation Inventory) in a private area.

The second meeting is arranged several days after the intake meeting. The PGP (Personal Goal Profile) is completed by the client and reviewed with the exercise professional. SMI scores are also available to the trainer by this time. At this session, long-term goals are set with the client. They are then divided into short-term goals and documented. After these tasks have been completed, the exercise professional gives clients a complete orientation to fitness center equipment and available classes and activities. While this is not an exercise prescription, enough directions should be given so that the client's safety is insured while exercising.

The exercise prescription meeting should be set for about one month after intake for clients scoring in the SMI ranges of one, two and three (see Chapter 4). This time is provided so

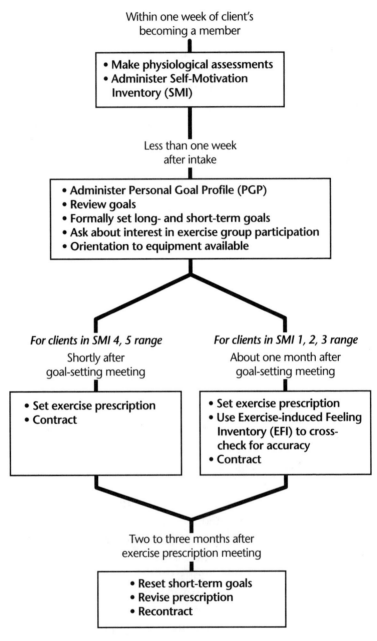

Figure 5.2. Time line for administration of MAP procedures.

that clients may develop exercise-type preference and establish maintainable intensity and frequency levels. Clients in SMI ranges of four and five do not present a large risk if an exercise prescription is established sooner. Often these clients become more frustrated waiting for their finalized workout, since they likely have established exercise preferences early. Again, though, with clients in the SMI one, two and three ranges, it is advisable to defer the exercise prescription about one month. These clients should be given a reminder phone call about one week before the exercise prescription appointment.

The exercise prescription meeting allows staff to develop an exercise routine based upon goals, self-motivation level, physiological indicators and client likes and dislikes. During this session, the client "tries out" the workout. Cross-checks for the prescription's appropriateness are made by using the EFI (Exercise-Induced Feeling Inventory) before and after the exercise session and by asking the client about his/her comfort with the workout. Changes are then made if necessary. After the prescription is finally established, the session ends with formal contracting (as outlined earlier). As the meeting concludes, a re-evaluation appointment is set for about two to three months.

Reevaluation appointments should be confirmed about one week prior. Reevaluation meetings allow the exercise professional and client to evaluate progress, re-set the exercise prescription, establish new short-term goals and recontract to the newly revised workout. Encourage variety and flexibility as clients start to make exercise part of their weekly routines. At the conclusion, establish a time for another reevaluation meeting in another two to three months. These followup sessions should be ongoing, especially for clients who scored in the SMI levels of one, two and three.

89

KEY FACT

11

To effectively implement your retention
program, specifically train staff for their
specialized roles. Each skill should be
learned, practiced separately and
coordinated into a coherent time frame.

The staff training process

Staff training is critical for successful implementation of your retention system. Until this book was published, I trained all personnel involved in the administration and delivery of MAP. Now, that task may be accomplished internally, with the possible use of some consulting, depending on your situation. Since each fitness center setting differs somewhat, it is important that administrators and directors reach a consensus regarding the particulars of training line staff. This will require meetings that outline: a) the number of training sessions required to cover relevant material, b) the length of sessions, c) whether sessions will include all trainers or be divided into several smaller sessions, d) the specific content of each meeting, and e) who will present the training, and in what format.

Although training of staff in the MAP Steps can be flexible, some constants should apply. For example, while the standard protocols of self-motivation assessment, goal-setting and the exercise prescription process can be taught in larger settings, the skills of applying motivation techniques (e.g., relapse prevention training, dissociation training) require small groups so that monitored role-play is possible. While group sessions allow efficient information transfer between directors and trainers, only real-life application and feedback can enable each professional to adapt the retention system to specific client concerns. Theory transfer, role-playing, answering questions and giving feedback regarding real-life skills application are all necessary to training staff in the retention techniques. Below are specific directives for each Step of the system.

STEP 1. ASSESSING THE MEMBER/ANTICIPATING NEEDS

This step requires training in the use of the SMI. Since this is an easy instrument to administer and score, directions

91

from the copyright holder will largely be self-explanatory. Staff should learn to introduce the SMI as a means to aid client success, and be able to review results with clients in a positive manner. For example, if a client scores in the "two" range, his/her lack of motivation should not be emphasized; rather, the state-of-the-art techniques that will help facilitate success should be accentuated. Trainers should be aware of the implications *and limitations* of the SMI, as was stated in the previous chapter. Exercise professionals should each complete and score their own SMI.

STEP 2. ESTABLISHING CLIENT GOALS

Establishing goals requires that the trainer be familiar with the use of the PGP. Each professional should self-administer this tool to become aware of its nuances. Trainers should be aware of how to present this instrument in a positive manner to clients, as well as be able to explain its usefulness to them. Training in setting long-and short-term goals, based on SMI and PGP results, should be provided.

Since clients often wish for goals that are difficult (or

Clients often wish for goals that are difficult (or impossible) to attain, short-term.

impossible) to attain, short-term, exercise professionals should develop skills necessary to negotiate manageable and meaningful goals. Some role-playing experience should be provided that allows trainers to practice: a) citing appropriate goals based on clients' individual make-up, and b) negotiating suitable goals with over-eager clients. Finally, the procedure of documenting goals on exercise cards should be reviewed.

STEP 3. DEVELOPING AND CONTRACTING TO AN EXERCISE PRESCRIPTION

The exercise prescription production must be trained for in some detail. The trainer should receive guidance in how to synthesize client information in the areas of physiological condition, motivational level, goals set and time availability for developing appropriate exercise prescriptions. He/she should be able to effectively counter clients' initial desire to rush progress, and educate them in the validity of manageable exercise as part of their general lifestyle. Again, role-playing is an effective way to supplement training for this skill.

Training in EFI should include application practice. The exercise professional must be able to effectively gain information to judge the appropriateness of an exercise prescription. If the prescription does not fulfill client needs, an ability to adjust that prescription, without allowing the client to perceive it as failure, is essential.

Trainers should be made familiar with *all* activities that clients may avail themselves of within your facility. The importance of freedom of activity choice must be made clear. Finally, the contracting process should be trained for specifically. Trainers should have the ability to communicate to clients the importance of maintaining their agreed-upon commitment. The balance between flexibility of program and maintaining commitment must be conveyed.

STEP 4. GOAL/PROGRESS MONITORING

Trainers should be taught how to advocate for consistent client self-tracking on the exercise cards. Chapter 4 made clear the necessity of facilitating such self-feedback. Role-playing should be utilized to develop techniques that effectively remind clients of this need. Exercise professionals should be able to explain to clients each part of the tracking process. Make certain *all* trainers are clear with each part of the exercise card, so that they may revise and clarify sections for clients.

Trainers should be able to emphasize to clients gains that are symbolized through self-tracking. A link between exercise and goal attainment must be projected to clients at all times. Exercise professionals should be given training in how to encourage clients to use all elements of self-feedback (e.g., standardized charts, exercise cards) for their motivational benefit.

When meeting with a client individually, trainers should be able to provide progress feedback in a realistic but extremely positive manner. In addition to role-play training, supervisor feedback based on actual in-progress applications is helpful. As in most of the previously stated interventions, teaching by example or "modeling" is an extremely effective technique.

STEPS 5 AND 6. ENHANCING AND REPAIRING MOTIVATION

The skills required for each intervention of Steps 5 and 6 require specific, directed education. These will usually require the most time in training because exercise professionals usually have not had *any* training in the psychological aspects associated with exercise persistence. Many staff members will initially be uncomfortable in unfamiliar areas. This is an area in which outside help is often useful.

Each specific technique should be broken down into its

most basic parts. Copies of notes, which may be referred to in the future, are also of help in the delivery of this information. Concentrate on maintaining small, interactive sessions when developing the enhance-and-repair motivation skills in trainers. Role-play exercises are a must.

To give an example, the repair motivation technique of "relaxation" may be trained as follows:

• Train the professional in the signs of bodily tension that may suggest the use of relaxation training.

• Train how to initiate the relaxation training process with the client.

• Train in the specific components of the intervention, as suggested in Chapter 4.

• Allow the exercise professional to role-play relaxation training with an associate.

• Present him/her helpful, encouraging feedback.

• Monitor the technique's use with an actual client and present feedback.

Enhance-and-repair techniques (reviewed in detail in Chapter 4) are not difficult to learn, but are usually different from what exercise trainers are familiar with. Remind them that they are not expected to be "psychologists," and assure them that their efforts will be greatly useful to clients in eliminating, or significantly reducing, common barriers to continued exercise. Again, allow enough time for training each technique so that trainers' on-floor, circulation time may be put to best use.

Motivation of staff

Compared with usual fitness center methods, your staff will be called upon to complete considerably more and different tasks. Most trainers find these new and interesting responsibilities rewarding. Be sure to validate the importance of their work. Let them know their professional endeavors are associated with clients' long-term success and all of the mental and physical positives that are associated with that success. Challenge staff to undertake their new responsibilities effectively. Be certain that a work ethic of client service and concern is central within your fitness center. Be willing to model the delivery of each of MAP's elements to clients yourself.

Although staff may develop bonds with clients with whom they are especially comfortable interacting, make certain they know the "at-risk" client is their primary concern. Most fitness centers have only a limited number of staff circulating among exercisers. Their main responsibility should be to clients appearing overly-challenged, uncomfortable and/or disoriented within their exercise setting. Although "spotting" a habitual exerciser while bench pressing may be of use, time spent with a client struggling with persistence due to his/her discomfort with the treadmill, may be more productive.

Train your staff to prioritize their valuable on-floor time so that it will produce the most effective results. Emphasize the absolute need to enable as many clients as possible to adopt exercise into their lifestyles. Incorporate both this general philosophical approach and specific, directed training into your retention program implementation process.

Adjusting to special needs

Certainly, exercise prescriptions will vary greatly based upon individuals' physiological conditions. Special care needs to be given to: a) people with coronary heart disease, b) post-myocardial infarction clients, c) obese individuals, and d) clients with orthopedic problems. This section, however, will be limited to the *exercise adherence* implications of clients with special needs. Clients presenting with problems that staff is not trained and/or credentialed to cope with must be referred to a qualified professional. The importance of selectively using outside professionals was reviewed in the

Repairing Motivation section of Chapter 4.

CLIENTS WITH HEART CONDITIONS

Although exercise prescriptions must be appropriately adapted, most MAP treatments require little modification for these special clients. In fact, much of the research on which MAP is based utilized samples from the "normal" population *and* heart patients. Although clients with heart conditions do not have as wide a choice as others in developing their exercise prescriptions (because of their physiological limitations), they have a built-in motivator to compensate (the knowledge that specific exercise patterns may be *essential* to their longevity). While coronary patients do not have different dropout rates when compared to other clients, they are certainly excellent candidates for improvement when presented with the advantages of your new retention system.

MOTIVATIONAL DIFFERENCES

Most of the practical parts of this book have presented

A highly self-motivated individual may view the muscle soreness after a hard workout as a sign of accomplishment.

KEY FACT

12

Since needs and perceptions of positives

and negatives vary with age,

implementation of retention elements must

reflect age-specific concerns.

methods intended to strengthen the exercise behavior through clients' association of exercise with positive experience. Similarly, attempts have been made to minimize discomforts, barriers and punishers. As you have already seen, self-motivation is a variable that can often dictate individuals' interpretation of what is, and is not, rewarding. A highly self-motivated individual may view the muscle soreness after a hard workout as a sign of accomplishment. A low-motivated individual may perceive the same soreness as intolerable and seek a quick escape from it (dropout). A constant awareness of how motivation affects interpretation must be maintained. Similarly, age plays a major part in what is reinforcing and what is punishing to the individual. It is important to be sensitive to age differences when applying many of the aspects of your retention system.

CHILDREN

Youngsters generally seek out fun. They are usually not concerned about long-term, healthful behaviors, and do not connect exercise with their assuming responsibility for their health. Therefore, methods that seek to reinforce children through educating them in the validity of exercise may not be very useful. Stress management is also not of much interest to youth.

Rewards for exercising should come from its social, energizing and sometimes competitive effect. When done in an understandable fashion, goal setting and self-reinforcement can be productive treatments. As children move into their teens, programming for effective peer group support can be especially useful for promoting retention.

YOUNG ADULTS

These clients have just recently completed college and are in their 20s. Many are hopeful that exercise will enhance their attractiveness. Weight control is often a primary concern. Since many are initially entering the work force, exercise is often used as an "energy release" at the end of the day. Programming for this age group should anticipate their needs.

Since this group is often goal-oriented, goat setting/contracting procedures will work especially well. For young adults, it is important to effectively regulate the exercise prescription. Since their work world often demands quick results, this may carry over to their exercise endeavors. Be certain to balance these clients' desire for productivity with their need for exercise to be a stress-free, refreshing experience.

MID-ADULTS

These clients range in age from their 30s to their 50s. Many have family responsibilities and derive many rewards from their work and family. Often, their role as a support system to the family results in a short supply of time. Exercise may take a low priority for this group, due to its association with low-importance leisure pursuits.

Educational approaches, which stress the importance of exercise for health, are useful for this population. Also, techniques that allow these clients to distance themselves, however briefly, from outside demands (e.g., imagery, relaxation) should increase exercise palatability. Emphasize to these members that they should feel entitled to set self-improvement goals and allocate sufficient time in their busy schedules to reach them.

OLDER ADULTS

For clients 60 and over, exercise serves to: a) slow physical declines, b) enhance physical self-image and c) provide a social outlet. Since this group often has considerable time in which to workout, facilitation of social support works extremely well. A special sensitivity toward exercise prescriptions is necessary due to frequent injuries and often declining physical capabilities.

Programming should provide for self-monitoring and goal setting, but should include prescription flexibility contingencies. This should not be overlooked due to day-to-day fluctuations in their individual reactions to physical intensity levels. Be certain to enable these clients to associate exercise with rejuvenated feelings, rather than fatigue and physical taxation.

Summary

This chapter reviewed MAP system implementation concerns not covered in Chapter 4. Because coordination of professional roles is important within the fitness center, the respective responsibilities of managers, department heads and exercise leaders/trainers were outlined. Since each has a vital role in transferring exercise psychology research knowledge into client successes, each role and its specific contribution to the MAP retention system was detailed.

Managers need to facilitate the development of staff training sessions and evaluate and refine the effectiveness of the program's implementation. Fitness center department heads must take responsibility for training staff and be especially concerned that the new methods effectively reach the client when most needed — when preparing exercise programming and during exercise sessions. Exercise professionals and trainers must be fluent in each element of the retention system. They must also know how to individually adapt and appropriately utilize techniques for those in need.

A time frame for implementing the MAP Steps with clients was also presented. The initial client-trainer meeting provides the best time to assess client motivation, after baseline physiological and risk data are taken. Shortly after, a second individual session allows for goal setting and an orientation to the exercise activities available. After several weeks to a month (for somewhat at-risk clients), exercise preferences and time availabilities can most accurately be noted. A meeting at this time finalizes short- and long-term client goals and allows for a tryout of a preliminary exercise prescription (while testing for its psychological accuracy). It also calls upon the client to commit or "contract" to their established workout. Future follow-up meetings are set so that progress may be tracked and new short-term goals set.

The staff training process was next reviewed, giving some specific educational suggestions advisable for each of the MAP Steps. An emphasis was placed on information transfer, role-playing exercises, teaching by example and supervisor feedback of staff performances with clients. In utilizing the various assessment instruments incorporated in MAP, exercise professionals need to be confident in their administration and interpretation as well as in presenting a rationale for their use to clients. Training in the techniques of goal-setting, contracting and establishing and documenting an exercise prescription enables trainers to quickly synthesize specific client information and be effective in negotiating appropriate, individualized protocols for each member. The ability for staff to recognize the signs of exercise-based discomforts, and usefully intervene, requires strong social as well as technical skills. Role-playing, in addition to constant, constructive supervisor feedback is essential after exercise professionals have been thoroughly schooled in the varied helping skills.

In addition, methods directed at motivating staff were focused upon in this chapter. Since trainers hold much greater responsibilities within the MAP system than within "traditional" fitness center environments, providing a rewarding and interesting experience for them is important. Staff should be challenged to view their role as client success facilitators, and be trained to prioritize their time to attain these ends.

Finally, adjusting programming to clients' special needs was addressed. Those with physical conditions and limitations often require special adaptations to maintain a positive outlook on exercising. Different age groups often perceive the exercise experience differently. For instance, children gain their exercise-based rewards from its energizing, social and sometimes competitive potentials. Young adults are often concerned with exercise's effect on their appearance and/or its use as an energy release at the end of a workday. Middle-aged adults may look to exercise as a tension-release and connect its worth with its potential for physical productivity and disease prevention. Older adults may also see exercise as a means to facilitate a better physical self, an enhanced self-image and as a social outlet. Programming must be sensitive to these special needs.

Chapter 6 will serve to consolidate your new knowledge about client exercise behavior, as well as recap previously presented research findings regarding exercise adherence enhancement and their applications with your members.

6

A new direction for retention success

KEEPING YOUR MEMBERS exercising is a win-win situation. It positively impacts the physical and mental well-being of members, and improves your professional and financial success. But until now, the fitness-services industry has not put into use retention tools that are based on empirical research findings. In fact, while citing attrition as its major concern, the industry's attempts to counter dropout have often relied upon unsophisticated methods. A focus on registering new members, in place of dropouts, has masked attrition. Sometimes, the occasional motivational gimmick has distorted perceptions, allowing beliefs that real retention efforts *are* being made. The industry should not be criticized for lack of effort; but, it has failed to use available scientific knowledge to direct retention efforts.

Frequently, when a client drops out, follow-up phone calls are made, and general inquiries include: "Was there a problem with the staff?" and "Were the classes too large, or too noisy?" While such questions are well-meaning, they miss the point entirely when exercise adherence is the concern. Although unmotivated clients tend not to reveal their reasons for dropout, it often has to do with continual, unpleasant feelings created by the exercise sessions. Possibly, some members are overly self-conscious about their bodies. For others, exercise may have created an unpleasant muscle soreness, or it may have become a lonely, uncomfortable endeavor yielding little or no results. Clients have rarely been helped to develop what is needed to successfully adapt to an often challenging task.

The need for a retention system

The position of this book is to systematically direct your retention efforts to the heart of clients' exercise barriers and discomforts. Motivationally challenged clients *can* succeed when well-directed efforts focus on the critical variables that turn their failure into success. While a smiling reception staff and a clean, cheerful facility are essential, they will usually not make the difference between long-term retention and rapid dropout. Isolating, and effectively treating, the multitude of personal, adaptive variables proven to affect exercise adherence is what will make the big difference.

The Steps of the MAP system will help you affect *real* results. No longer will administrators be limited to addressing insignificant, peripheral elements of the retention process. They can now specifically focus on the critical aspects that yield client/exercise success through easily implemented, directed staff efforts. Clients need not be "blamed" for their lack of motivation and, consequently, lost as members. They can now have their limited motivation enhanced and nurtured. Exercise can be transformed from a burden to a rejuvenating, social experience that leads to a continual sense of mastery and accomplishment. The use of a psychologically based system maximizes your chances of enhancing client motivation to the point where exercise becomes a habit — a pleasant, productive behavior that is willingly fit into each week *at your facility*.

The basis of an effective system

In earlier chapters, you have learned about the theories of exercise behavior, as well as the known individual variables that affect exercise adoption and persistence. Your new knowledge relating to these areas enables you to understand the highly individual basis of exercise behaviors. You now know the factors that will help individualize your service to clients (e.g., self-motivation level, goals, age group), so that appropriate attention and efforts may be given to maximize each one's success (and yours).

You are also now aware of the extensive research contributions dealing with methods to prevent exercise dropout. Berger and McInman (1993), in their careful review of this body of work, have concluded that adherence methods should: a) include exercisers in decision making, b) adopt flexible exercise standards, c) set reasonable and obtainable goals, d) provide moderate exercise prescriptions, e) establish regularity of workouts, f) de-emphasize competition, g) provide feedback, h) cultivate support systems, and i) ensure effective leadership. By following this book, your retention system will incorporate these important concerns. In fact, your system will enable results to be taken a step further than the studies.

Research experiments generally do not consider the influences of individual characteristics known to affect dropout. Since you will obtain a substantial, individualized profile of each client's motivational level, goals and exercise likes and dislikes, your efforts will be better directed. What you will have is the best available retention system — a thorough screening of clients' psychological predispositions to shape and optimize your retention techniques.

KEY FACT

13

To maximize fitness center member
retention, the use of a formal system,
sensitive to the many physical and
psychological client differences, works best.
The system should be easily applied, and be
based on the best available research
findings. It should serve the needs of
administrators and exercise leaders, as well
as clients.

The advantages of a systematic approach

This book emphasizes the systematic use of fitness center member retention methods. A system, as opposed to a hodge-podge of ideas randomly applied as the need might seem apparent, has many advantages. For the administrator, a coherent system is able to be checked for appropriate usage across exercise professionals. Since the staff is trained in a uni-fied manner, methods can be applied when and where they are needed. Directives have been built into the MAP system, which adapt its many elements to individualized needs. Administrators are able to easily maintain quality control of all parts of their new, comprehensive program.

For exercise professionals, a systematic retention pro-gram allows them to build upon their physiological knowl-edge and greatly enhance their worth as an exercise leader. New knowledge gained about the psychological aspects of exercise adherence, and how such methods may be best applied, revitalizes job interest and satisfaction. Along with instituting correct exercise procedures, an ability to affect meaningful, lifelong changes in personal exercise habits becomes an interesting, central focus of the exercise profes-sional's practice.

For the client, your retention system enables those who would drop out to succeed. From the start, clients' needs are individually addressed. Initially, their personalized needs are appraised through the assessment of motivational levels and goals. They are then guided through the development of, and commitment to, an appropriate exercise program. You contin-ually reevaluate, revise and generally assist them in assimilat-ing exercise into their lives. They are provided with self-help techniques, as well as outside support systems, that maximize their chances for long-term success. In the long run, exercise barriers and discomforts are transformed. A more healthful lifestyle becomes the outcome for them. Increased profession-al productivity becomes the outcome for you. The time taken to learn and carefully implement the MAP systematic approach reaps its benefits for all involved.

Conclusion

Keeping clients coming back is essential to the success of any fitness center. You have been shown, through this book, the theoretical and research bases for developing an effective retention program, as well as the means for applying these techniques at your facility. The corporate, insurance and health maintenance communities are beginning to realize what you have probably known for some time — that exercise is as tightly linked to preventive medicine as it is to enhancing clients' outward appearances and self-esteem. Only through regular exercise can your members' psychological well-being be enhanced, their aging process be more rewarding, their sense of mastery be increased and their self-confidence improved.

Through facilitating these important accomplishments, you will increase your own professionalism, as well as significantly increase the overall success of your facility. I hope you have come to realize the need for tapping into the relevant research findings, and systematically using them to maximize your and your members' successes. Members' appraisals of their exercise experiences are the key to their retention. When you, your staff and your clients are equipped with the best tools, and utilize them in a consistent, logical fashion, large-scale, long-term exercise maintenance is virtually ensured.

I hope your thoughtful use of the ideas and techniques that I have presented in this book causes you great personal satisfaction. Be assured that your important undertaking will positively affect many.

Appendix A

Exercise card sample

Name _____

Sex _____ Age _____ Eval. Date _____

Target Heart Zone _____ I Code: _____

Health History:
K   CV   A   Orth: _____
D   BP   S   Other _____

GOALS

Goal & Program	Strength	Aerobic	B.F.	Flex	Weight	Contract
Long-term Goals						Staff:
Short-term Goals						
Exercise Prescription						Member:

WORKOUT

ACTIVITY Date:						
Warm-Up/Stretch						
Aerobic Class						
CV Equipment						
Strength Machines/FW						
Swimming						
Racquet Sport						

PROGRESS TRACKING

Tracking Factors	Intake	Reeval. #1	Reeval. #2	Reeval. #3
VO2 max				
Flexibility				
Body Fat				
Weight				
Strength				

Appendix B

Personal Goal Profile directions

Here at _____, we are especially interested in helping you get exactly what you want from your workout programs. Since individual goals vary greatly (i.e., from fine-tuning one's body for high-caliber athletic competition, to just feeling better physically and mentally), we have chosen an information-gathering method — the **Personal Goal Profile** — to design exactly the right program for you. Here's how it works.

We have suggested some possible items that may represent your fitness goals. There are spaces to add items that are not included, but may be important to you. You are encouraged to fill in items in the spaces provided to help us tailor a program to your needs. When filling out your **Personal Goal Profile**, we use "10" as the number to strive for; 10 means fully reaching that particular goal.

First, decide which items are important to you, then draw a line across from each of your items to *indicate where you feel you are now*. Do nothing with the items that are not important to you. Place a star next to the items that are especially important to you.

At the bottom of this page is an example of a completed form. This person has indicated several goals by drawing a line next to them. The end of each line shows where that person believes he or she is now. For instance, this person feels that on a scale of 1 to 10, he or she is a 5 in terms of weight control, but a 2 in terms of stress management. A star next to stress management has been drawn by this individual to show that it is an especially important goal.

The professionals who help in designing your program will use your information to: 1) help break down your goals into "short-term" goals, 2) suggest useful activities to help you move toward your "long-term" goals and 3) monitor your progress and recommend changes when necessary.

We feel that if you commit to your goal, you will reach it. The **Personal Goal Profile** is one important tool to help us help you.

Please complete your profile on the next page. Don't spend too much time with any individual item, as the profile provides merely a general impression of you. As progress is made and goals change, we will revisit them during future reevaluations and revise your **Personal Goal Profile** as needed.

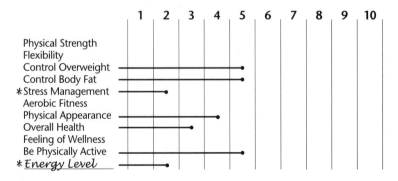

Appendix C

Personal Goal Profile (PGP)

Personal Goal Profile

	Far from reaching goal									**Goal has been attained**
	1	2	3	4	5	6	7	8	9	10
Physical Strength										
Flexibility										
Control Overweight										
Control Body Fat										
Stress Management										
Aerobic Fitness										
Physical Appearance										
Overall Health										
Feeling of Wellness										
Be Physically Active										
_____										
_____										
_____										
_____										

113

Appendix D

The Exercise-Induced Feeling Inventory (EFI)

Instructions: Please use the following scale to indicate the extent to which each word below describes *how you feel at this moment in time*. Record your responses by filling in the appropriate circle next to each word.

> 0 = Do Not Feel (DNF)
> 1 = Feel Slightly
> 2 = Feel Moderately
> 3 = Feel Strongly
> 4 = Feel Very Strongly (FVS)

	DNF 0 1 2 3 4 FVS		DNF 0 1 2 3 4 FVS
1. Refreshed	○ ○ ○ ○ ○	7. Happy	○ ○ ○ ○ ○
2. Calm	○ ○ ○ ○ ○	8. Tired	○ ○ ○ ○ ○
3. Fatigued	○ ○ ○ ○ ○	9. Revived	○ ○ ○ ○ ○
4. Enthusiastic	○ ○ ○ ○ ○	10. Peaceful	○ ○ ○ ○ ○
5. Relaxed	○ ○ ○ ○ ○	11. Worn-out	○ ○ ○ ○ ○
6. Energetic	○ ○ ○ ○ ○	12. Upbeat	○ ○ ○ ○ ○

Scoring for the Exercise-Induced Feeling Inventory (EFI)

The EFI consists of four distinct subscales. Subscale scores are obtained by summing the numerical values chosen for the adjectives within a particular subscale. The four subscales include: 1) Positive Engagement (items 4, 7 & 12), 2) Revitalization (items 1, 6 & 9), 3) Tranquility (items 2, 5 & 10) and 4) Physical Exhaustion (items 3, 8 & 11).

Source: "The Exercise-Induced Feeling Inventory: Development and Initial Validation" by Lise Gauvin and W. Jack Rejeski, *Journal of Sport and Exercise Psychology* (Vol. 15, No. 4), p. 409. Copyright 1993 by Human Kinetics Publishers. Reprinted by permission.

Glossary

anxiety. The fear, apprehension and/or worry emanating from a perception of threat.

balance sheet. A document in which perceived pros and cons relative to a specific behavior are recorded.

barriers (to exercise). Factors that oppose individuals' participation in exercise (e.g., lack of time, discomfort).

behavioral psychology. The branch of social science that uses visible behaviors to analyze psychological processes. It seeks to help individuals through the manipulation of outward actions.

cardiovascular exercise. Physical exertion stressing the heart and blood vessels.

cognitive-behavioral psychology. The branch of social science that analyzes outward behaviors through inner processes (e.g., thoughts, motivations).

cognitive restructuring. A technique in which an individual reinterprets his/her negative self-talk.

cohesion (group). The sense of unification, camaraderie and oneness that group processes often provide.

contracting. A formalized agreement to perform a specified task (e.g., a prescribed amount/type of exercise).

Cooper aerobic point system. A system, developed by Dr. Kenneth Cooper, for converting many types of exercises, activities and intensities into a unified scale.

dissociation. The technique of using intentional distractions to block physical sensations (often discomforts).

exercise adherence. Persistence in maintaining a regular exercise program.

exercise adherence strategies. Specific techniques designed to maximize persistence with an exercise program (e.g., goal setting, progress tracking).

exercise prescription. A recommendation for a specific course of exercise based on an individual's goals and fitness level. It usually includes type of exercise, duration, frequency and intensity level.

exercise psychology. The branch of social science that seeks to explain individuals' mental and behavioral processes related to exercise.

external reinforcer. Anything coming from outside one's self (e.g., compliments, money) that results in the likelihood that a behavior will occur in the future.

feedback system. A method in which past personal and/or group performances may be reviewed. Sometimes this information is modified or enhanced by others (e.g., exercise professionals).

goal setting. The establishment of a desired endpoint for which to strive.

habit formation. When a behavior (in this case, exercise) becomes routine or a matter of course.

imagery. The psychological technique of purposefully visualizing something within one's mind.

internal reinforcer. Anything coming from inside one's self (e.g., thoughts, perceptions) that causes a behavior to become more likely to occur in the future.

intervention. A purposeful strategy or technique designed to cause change.

mastery. An individual's perception of control over a skill or skills.

Member Adherence Program (MAP). System for implementing multiple, psychologically-based exercise adherence strategies; designed to maximize fitness center member retention.

motivation. Psychological state causing an individual to act.

physical self-estimation. An individual's self-judgment of his/her body.

psychological assessment. Technique of measuring one or more aspects of an individual's psychological makeup (e.g., questionnaire, interview).

psychosocial. The combination of internal (mental) and interactive (social) processes.

rationalization. The process of devising an acceptable reason, usually in self-deceit.

reinforcement. Anything happening after a behavior that makes that behavior more likely to occur in the future.

relapse prevention. The technique used to prepare individuals for "slips" that may occur in their established routine.

resistance training (exercise). Physical exertion requiring a muscle to work against force (usually weights).

retention (member). The maintenance of members. The avoidance of drop-out.

self-concept. An individual's perception of his/her self.

self-efficacy. An individual's judgment of his/her ability to perform certain actions (e.g., moderate exercise).

self-esteem. An individual's perception of his/her own value.

self-monitoring. Recording, tracking and reviewing of one's own (exercise) behaviors.

self-motivation. The general disposition causing an individual to act without the help of outside forces.

self-reinforcement. The provision of reward to one's self (usually for completing a desired behavior).

self-talk. The inner dialogue that an individual has with his/her self. It may be positive or negative.

social pressures. Coercion emanating from individuals other than one's self.

social support. Encouragement provided by individuals and/or groups (e.g., spouse, family).

stimulus control. A technique that establishes prompts or "triggers" that initiate a behavior (e.g., setting out exercise clothes at night to initiate morning workouts).

support systems. Groups (e.g., co-workers, family) that provide encouragement.

theoretical models of exercise. Scientific systems that attempt to explain exercise-related behavior through a limited amount of unique assumptions.

thought-stopping. A psychological technique used to abruptly stop negative statements to one's self (negative self-talk).

tracking system. A method to record information over time (e.g., aspects of individuals' previous exercise sessions).

trait. A distinguishing characteristic of an individual that tends to be enduring and resistant to change over time.

verbal persuasion. The use of words to cause an individual to believe something.

vicarious experience. The sense of a particular action through others actually performing it.

References

Ajzen, I. (1985). From intentions to actions: A theory of planned behavior. In J. Kuhl & J. Beckman (Eds.), *Action control: From cognition to behavior* (pp. 11-39). New York: Springer/Verlag.

Ajzen, I., & Fishbein, M. (1980). *Understanding attitudes and predicting social behavior*. Englewood Cliffs, NJ: Prentice Hall.

American College of Sports Medicine. (1986). *Guidelines for exercise testing and prescription*. Philadelphia: Lea & Febiger.

Andrews, G.M., Oldridge, N.B., Parker, J.O., Cunningham, D.A., Rechnitzer, P.A., Jones, N.L., Buck, C., Kavanagh, T., Shephard, R.J., Sutton, J.R., & McDonald, W. (1981). Reasons for dropout from exercise programs in post-coronary patients. *Medicine and Science in Sports and Exercise*, 13, 164-168.

Annesi, J.J. (1994). *Exercise adherence in fitness settings: A program for member retention*. Woodbridge, NJ: Enhanced Performance Technologies.

Atkins, C.J., Kaplan, R.M., Timms, R.M., Reinsch, S., & Lofback, K. (1984). Behavioral exercise programs in the management of chronic obstructive pulmonary disease. *Journal of Consulting and Clinical Psychology*, 52, 591-603.

Bandura, A. (1977). Self-efficacy: Toward a unifying theory of behavioral change. *Psychological Review*, 84, 191-215.

Bandura, A. (1986). *Social foundations of thought and action: A social cognitive theory*. Englewood Cliffs, NJ: Prentice Hall.

Belisle, M., Roskies, E., & Levesque, J.M. (1987). Improving adherence to physical activity. *Health Psychology*, 6, 159-172.

Berger, B.G., & McInman, A. (1993). Exercise and the quality of life. In R.N. Singer, M. Murphey, & L.K. Tennant (Eds.), *Handbook of research on sport psychology* (pp. 729-760). New York: Macmillan.

Borg, G. (1985). *An introduction to Borg's RPE-Scale*. New York: Mouvement.

Carron, A.V., & Spink, K.S. (1992). Internal consistency of the Group Environment Questionnaire modified for an exercise setting. *Perceptual and Motor Skills*, 74, 304-306.

Carron, A.V., & Spink, K.S. (1993). Team building in an exercise setting. *The Sport Psychologist*, 7, 8-18.

Carron, A.V., Widmeyer, W.N., & Brawley, L.R. (1988). Group cohesion and individual adherence to physical activity. *Journal of Sport & Exercise Psychology*, 10, 127-138.

Dishman, R.K. (1981). Biologic influences on exercise adherence. *Research Quarterly for Exercise and Sport*, 52, 143-159.

Dishman, R.K., & Gettman, L.R. (1980). Psychobiologic influences on exercise adherence. *Journal of Sport Psychology*, 2, 295-310.

Dishman, R.K., & Ickes, W. (1981). Self-motivation and adherence to therapeutic exercise. *Journal of Behavioral Medicine*, 4, 421-438.

Dishman, R.K., Ickes W., & Morgan, W.P. (1980). Self-motivation and adherence to habitual physical activity. *Journal of Applied Social Psychology*, 10, 115-132.

Duncan, T.E., Duncan S.C., & McAuley, E. (1993). The role of domain and gender-specific provisions of social relations in adherence to a prescribed exercise regimen. *Journal of Sport & Exercise Psychology*, 15, 220-231.

Epstein, L.H., Wing, R.R., Thompson, J.K., & Griffin, W. (1980). Attendance and fitness in aerobics exercise: The effects of contract and lottery procedures. *Behavior Modification*, 4, 465-479.

Fitterling, J.M., Martin, J.E., Gramling, S., Cole, P., & Milan, M.A. (1988). Behavioral management of exercise training in vascular headache patients: An investigation of exercise adherence and headache activity. *Journal of Applied Behavior Analysis*, 21, 9-19.

Gauvin, L., & Rejeski, W.J. (1993). The Exercise Induced Feeling Inventory: Development and initial validation. *Journal of Sport & Exercise Psychology*, 15, 403-423.

Heinzelman, F., & Bagley, R.W. (1970). Response to physical activity programs and their effects on health behavior. *Public Health Reports*, 85, 905-911.

Hoyt, M.F., & Janis, I.L. (1975). Increasing adherence to a stressful decision via a motivational balance-sheet procedure: A field experiment. *Journal of Personality and Social Psychology*, 31, 833-839.

IRSA (1993). The 1993 IRSA/Gallup Profiles of Success Series II — The athletic/fitness club industry. Boston, MA: Author.

Keefe, F.J., & Blumenthal, J.A. (1980). The Life Fitness Program: A behavioral approach to making exercise a habit. *Journal of Behavior Therapy and Experimental Psychiatry*, 11, 31-34.

King, A.C., & Frederiksen, L.W. (1984). Low-cost strategies for increasing exercise behavior. *Behavior Modification*, 8, 3-21.

King, A.C., Taylor, C.B., Haskell, W.L., & Debusk, R.F. (1988). Strategies for increasing early adherence to and long-term maintenance of home-based exercise training in healthy middle-aged men and women. *American Journal of Cardiology*, 61, 628-632.

Knapp, D.N. (1988). Behavioral management techniques and exercise promotion. In R.K. Dishman (Ed.), *Exercise adherence: Its impact on public health* (pp. 203-235). Champaign, IL: Human Kinetics.

Knapp, D., Gutmann, M., Foster, C., & Pollock, M. (1984). Self-motivation among 1984 Olympic speed skating hopefuls and emotional response and adherence to training. *Medicine and Science in Sports and Exercise*, 16, 114.

Locke, E.A., & Latham, G.P. (1985). The application of goal setting to sports. *Journal of Sport Psychology*, 7, 205-222.

Martin, J.E., Dubbert, P.M., Katell, A.D., Thompson, J.K., Razynski, J.R., Lake, M., Smith, P.D., Webster, J.S., Sikora, T., & Cohen, R.E. (1984). Behavioral control of exercise in sedentary adults: Studies 1 through 6. *Journal of Consulting and Clinical Psychology*, 52, 795-811.

Massie, J.F., & Shephard, R.J. (1971). Physiological and psychological effects of training. *Medicine and Science in Sports*, 3, 110-117.

McCready, M.L., & Long, B.C. (1985). Locus of control, attitudes toward physical activity, and exercise adherence. *Journal of Sport Psychology*, 7, 346-359.

McKenzie, T.L., & Rushall, B.S. (1974). Effects of self-recording on attendance and performance in a competitive swimming training environment. *Journal of Applied Behavioral Analysis*, 7, 199-206.

Nelson, J.K. (1978). Motivation effects of the use of norms and goals with endurance testing. *Research Quarterly*, 49, 317-321.

Noland, M.P., & Feldman, R.H.L. (1984). Factors related to the leisure exercise behavior of returning women college students. *Health Education*, 15, 32-36.

Oldridge, N.B. (1979). Compliance of post myocardial infarction patients to exercise programs. *Medicine and Science in Sports*, 11, 373-375.

Oldridge, N.B., Donner, A.P., Buck C.W., Jones, N.L., Andrew, G.M., Parker, J.O., Cunningham, D.A., Kavanagh, T., Rechnitzer, P.A., & Sutton, J.R. (1983). Predictors of dropout from cardiac exercise rehabilitation. *American Journal of Cardiology*, 51, 70-74.

Oldridge, N.B., & Jones, N.L. (1983). Improving patient compliance in cardiac exercise rehabilitation: Effects of written agreement and self-monitoring. *Journal of Cardiac Rehabilitation*, 3, 257-262.

Oldridge, N.B., & Spencer, J. (1983). Exercise habits and health perceptions after graduating or dropping out of cardiac rehabilitation. *Medicine and Science in Sports and Exercise*, 15, (Supplement), 120.

Pennebaker, J.W., & Lightner, J.M. (1980). Competition of internal and external information in an exercise setting. *Journal of Personality and Social Psychology*, 39, 165-174.

Pollock, M., Gettman, L., Milesis, C., Bah, M.D., Durstine, L., & Johnson, R.B. (1977). Effects of frequency and duration of training on attrition and incidence of injury. *Medicine and Science in Sports*, 9, 31-36.

Pollock, M.L., Wilmore, J.H., & Fox, S.M. (1984). *Exercise in health and disease: Evaluation and prescription for prevention and rehabilitation*. Philadelphia: W.B. Saunders.

Prochaska, J.O., & Marcus, B.H. (1994). The transtheoretical model: Applications to exercise. In R.K. Dishman (Ed.), *Advances in exercise adherence* (pp. 161-180). Champaign, IL: Human Kinetics.

Remers, L., Widmeyer, W.N., Williams, J.M., & Myers, L. (1995). Possible mediators and moderators of the class size member adherence relationship in exercise. *Journal of Applied Sport Psychology*, 7, 38-49.

Sallis, J.F., Haskell, W.L., Fortmann, M.S., Vranizan, K.M., Taylor, C.B., & Solomon, D.S. (1986). Predictors of adoption and maintenance of physical activity in a community sample. *Preventive Medicine*, 15, 331-341.

Spink, K.S., & Carron, A.V. (1993). The effects of team building on the adherence patterns of female exercise participants. *Journal of Sport & Exercise Psychology*, 15, 39-49.

Spink, K.S., & Carron, A.V. (1994). Group cohesion effects in exercise classes. *Small Group Research*, 25, 26-42.

Sonstroem, R.J. (1978). Physical estimation and attraction scales: Rationale and research. *Medicine and Science in Sports*, 10, 97-102.

Suinn, R.M. (1980). Body thinking: Psychology for Olympic champs. In R.M. Suinn (Ed.), *Psychology in sports: Methods and applications* (pp. 306-315). Minneapolis, MN: Burgess.

Thompson, C.E., & Wankel, L.M. (1980). The effects of perceived activity choice upon frequency of exercise behavior. *Journal of Applied Social Psychology*, 10, 436-443.

Thompson, J., Wyatt, J.T.B., & Craighead, L.W. (1984). Three theoretically based interventions to increase exercise adherence in a health-promotion regimen. *Psychosomatic Medicine*, 46, 80.

Triandis, H.C. (1977). *Interpersonal behavior*. Monterey, CA: Brooks/Cole.

United States Department of Health and Human Service, Public Health Service. (1991). *Healthy People 2000: National health promotion and disease. Prevention objectives*. Washington, DC: Government Printing Office.

Wankel, L.M. (1985). Personal and situational factors affecting exercise involvement: The importance of enjoyment. *Research Quarterly for Exercise and Sport*, 56, 275-282.

Wankel, L.M., & Thompson, C. (1977). Motivating people to be physically active: Self-persuasion vs. balanced decision making. *Journal of Applied Social Psychology*, 7, 332-340.

Wankel, L.M., Yardley, J.K., & Graham, J. (1985). The effects of motivational interventions upon the exercise adherence of high and low self-motivated adults. *Canadian Journal of Applied Sport Sciences*, 10, 147-156.

Weber, J., & Wertheim, E.H. (1989). Relationship of self-monitoring, special attention, body fat percentage, and self-motivation to attendance at a community gymnasium. *Journal of Sport & Exercise Psychology*, 11, 105-114.

Wysocki, T., Hall, G., Iwata, B., & Riordan, M. (1979). Behavioral management of exercise: Contracting for aerobic points. *Journal of Applied Behavior Analysis*, 12, 55-64.

Index